FIRST FROST

COZY FOLK KNITTING

LUCINDA GUY

INTERWEAVE.
interweave.com

Editor *Erica Smith*

Technical Editor *Therese Chynoweth*

Photographer *Joe Hancock*

Stylist *Anne Rocchio*

Hair and Makeup *Kathy MacKay*

Associate Art Director *Charlene Tiedemann*

Cover and Interior Design *Julia Boyles*

Layout Design *Connie Poole*

Production Designer *Kerry Jackson*

Interweave
A division of F+W Media, Inc.
4868 Innovation Drive
Fort Collins, CO 80525
interweave.com

Manufactured in China by RR Donnelley Shenzhen.

Library of Congress Cataloging-in-Publication Data
Guy, Lucinda, author.
First frost : cozy folk knitting / Lucinda Guy.

pages cm
Includes index.
ISBN 978-1-62033-336-5 (pbk.)
ISBN 978-1-62033-474-4 (PDF)
1. Knitting--Pattern. 2. Knitting--Europe, Northern. 3. Folk art--Europe, Northern. I. Title.
 TT819.E853G885 2014
 746.43'2041--dc23
                                    2014011105

10 9 8 7 6 5 4 3 2 1

contents

introduction

First Frost: Cozy Folk Knitting is a celebration of that certain time of the year when nights become longer, darker, and colder and dawn brings a bright, clear, and frosty morning. The seasons shift, summer has long gone, and there is a definite chill in the air. It is a time when you feel the need to light a fire in the fireplace and cheerful candles on your table, and reach for cozy woolen knits to wrap up in.

This collection also celebrates all that is wonderful about the construction of decorative folk knitting, in particular the construction of folk mittens, folk gloves, and folk socks. As essential everyday items for anyone living and working in the harsh, cold climates of the North, these folk knits could range from the simple and utilitarian to exuberantly textural, braided, tasseled, colored, and patterned knits traditionally reserved for special occasions and celebrations. These intriguing and beautifully decorative knitting techniques have served as inspiration for the twenty cozy and comforting designs in this book.

In traditional decorative Northern European folk knitting, a single pair of socks or mittens could easily have as many as ten, possibly more, individual folk motifs contained within its designs, and these garments were often further decorated with colorful fringing, tassels, and tufts.

What better way is there to celebrate these old and often ancient folk techniques than by continuing to incorporate them into our everyday knits? As you work your way through the patterns in this book you will become familiar with these fantastic techniques; and from that point on, whenever you decide to knit a pair of socks, you will know how to enhance them with various embellishments: bands of patterns, a knotted decorative cast-on, a tassel, or specific shaping at the toe. Every pair of mittens or gloves you knit could have a colorful, braided cast-on, colorful textural details, and patterns.

I hope you enjoy making and wearing these beautiful knits!

Lucinda Guy

folk colors

Tapio, the ancient protective Finnish forest spirit, was believed to have hair of lichen, eyebrows of moss, and a mossy green cloak. When asked, Tapio would benevolently grant safe journey through his forests.

The typical Nordic, Baltic, or Scandinavian folk palette consists of colors that were considered to be protective, symbolic, and important. Northern peasant life traditionally revolved around seasonal celebrations of growing and producing food; the colors considered highly significant and representative of nature and renewal were used prolifically: berry reds, natural white, bright sky blues, golden corn yellow, fresh leafy greens, and forest greens.

The most popular of these color combinations is red and white. Red was thought to symbolize the sun, fire, youth, and life, and white was associated with purity. When used in combination, red and white were considered portentous and were important for ritual celebrations such as marriage.

The natural tones of sheep's wool were used in combination with dyed yarn. Moss, bark, leaves, berries, lichens, and toadstools, readily available in the fields and forests, were used regularly for dyeing. In all of Northern folk art, woodlands and forests were held in great esteem by country people, and often closely associated with folklore and all things magical.

Over the past two hundred years chemical dyes that produce consistently clearer, brighter colors began to replace the local plant dyes, and distinct new color and pattern combinations emerged. These vibrant combinations are now universally associated with Northern folk knitwear.

TÓKA SOCKS

BEAUTIFUL EXAMPLES of folk socks and stockings can often be found in museums. These gorgeous garments can range from elegant one-colored Swedish twined stockings to elaborately patterned and colored Fair Isle socks. It is the riotously patterned and exuberantly colored knitted Estonian stockings from the Estonian island of Muhu that I turned to for reference for these socks.

The Tóka socks have been knitted in the round with 5 double-pointed needles from the top down using a traditional Estonian cast-on, colored rib patterning, and several bands of Estonian patterns. These have been embellished with duplicate stitches and French knots. There is a single flower motif on the foot to demonstrate the clever technique of knitting single areas of pattern in the round, and the toe is shaped using the distinctive Estonian toe shaping technique.

Traditionally, Estonian heels would have been knitted after the sock was completed, but I have designed the Tóka socks with a turned heel and shaped gusset.

FINISHED MEASUREMENTS
8½" (21.5 cm) foot circumference and 10¾" (27.5 cm) long.

YARN
Sock weight (#1 Super Fine).

Shown here: Cascade Heritage Sock Yarn (75% superwash merino wool, 25% nylon; 437 yd [399 m]/100 g): #5628 Cotton Candy (A), #5646 Pumpkin (B), #5606 Burgundy (C), #5612 Moss (D), 1 skein each.

NEEDLES
Set of 5 size U.S. 2 (2.75 mm) double-pointed (dpn).

Adjust needle size if necessary to obtain the correct gauge.

NOTIONS
Markers (m); waste yarn; tapestry needle.

GAUGE
30 sts and 42 rnds = 4" (10 cm) in St st worked in rounds, after washing.

Right Sock

With 1 strand of A and 2 strands of B, use the Knotted Cast-On method (see Techniques), CO 75 sts—76 sts, including the slipknot. Cut yarns, leaving long tails to use for braided cord. Divide sts over 4 dpn with 21 sts on Needle 1, 20 sts each on Needles 2 and 3, and 15 sts on Needle 4. Sl last st on Needle 1 to Needle 4, pass last st CO over the slipped st and off needle—75 sts. Place marker (pm) and join for working in rnds.

Next rnd: With A, knit into the back of each st.

Next rnd: *K4, p1; rep from * around.

Rep last rnd twice more.

Work Rows 1–68 of Leg chart—62 sts rem.

Heel

Next row (RS): K16, turn.

Next row: Sl 1, p31, turn. Place rem 30 sts onto one needle or waste yarn for instep.

Work back and forth on rem 32 sts for heel.

Work Rows 1–32 of Right Heel chart.

Shape Heel

Row 1 (RS): K18, skp, k1, turn.

Row 2 (WS): Sl 1, p5, p2tog, p1, turn.

Row 3: Sl 1, k6, skp, k1, turn.

Row 4: Sl 1, p7, p2tog, p1, turn.

LEG

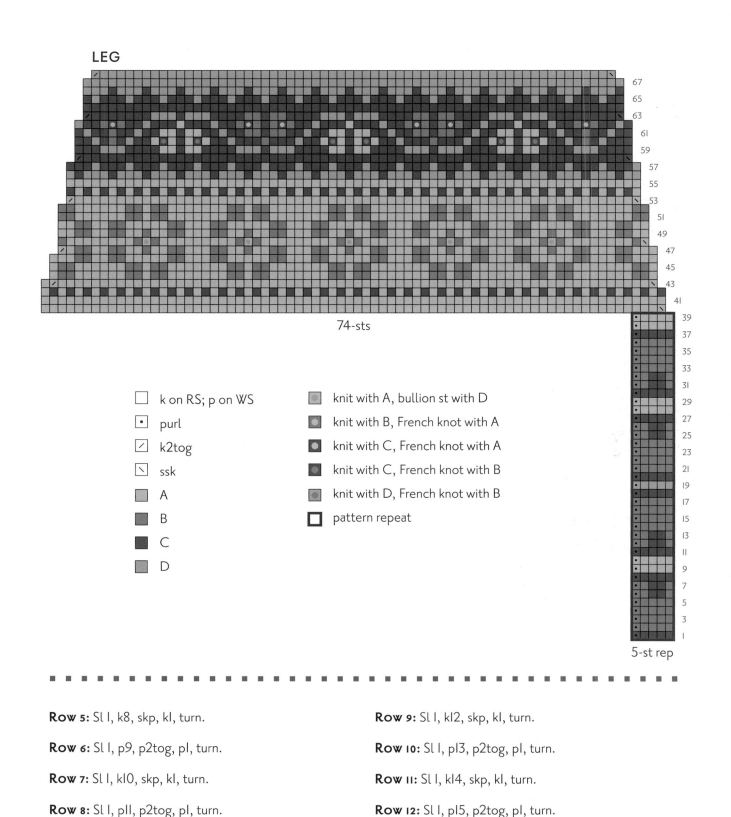

74-sts

5-st rep

- [ ] k on RS; p on WS
- [•] purl
- [⟋] k2tog
- [⟍] ssk
- A
- B
- C
- D

- knit with A, bullion st with D
- knit with B, French knot with A
- knit with C, French knot with A
- knit with C, French knot with B
- knit with D, French knot with B
- [ ] pattern repeat

Row 5: Sl 1, k8, skp, k1, turn.

Row 6: Sl 1, p9, p2tog, p1, turn.

Row 7: Sl 1, k10, skp, k1, turn.

Row 8: Sl 1, p11, p2tog, p1, turn.

Row 9: Sl 1, k12, skp, k1, turn.

Row 10: Sl 1, p13, p2tog, p1, turn.

Row 11: Sl 1, k14, skp, k1, turn.

Row 12: Sl 1, p15, p2tog, p1, turn.

FOOT

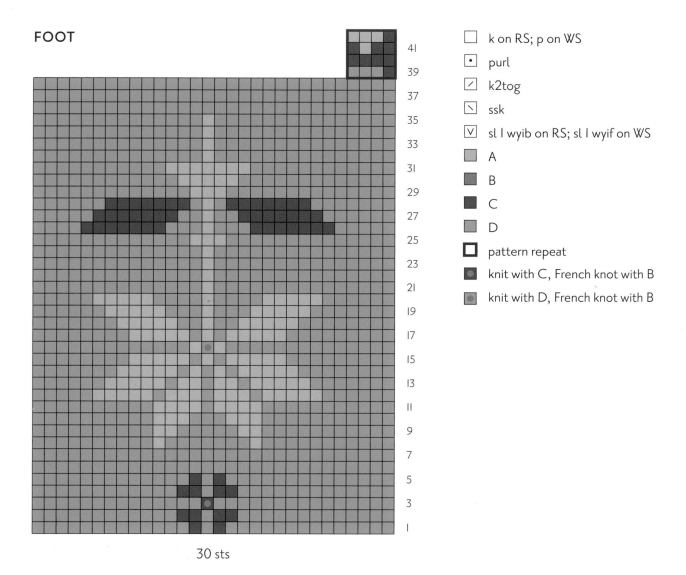

41
39
37
35
33
31
29
27
25
23
21
19
17
15
13
11
9
7
5
3
1

30 sts

☐ k on RS; p on WS

· purl

☑ k2tog

◩ ssk

☑ sl 1 wyib on RS; sl 1 wyif on WS

▨ A

▨ B

■ C

▨ D

☐ pattern repeat

● knit with C, French knot with B

● knit with D, French knot with B

Row 13: Sl 1, k16, skp, turn.

Row 14: Sl 1, p16, p2tog, turn—18 sts rem.

Row 15: K9.

Gusset

With D and using dpn, Needle 1, knit rem 9 heel sts, pick up and knit 16 sts along edge of heel; Needles 2 and 3, knit across the held 30 instep sts; Needle 4,

pick up and knit 16 sts along rem edge of heel, knit the rem 9 heel sts—80 sts.

Distribute sts if necessary with 25 sts (9 heel sts and 16 gusset sts) each on Needles 1 and 4, and 15 instep sts each on Needles 2 and 3. Pm for beg of rnd and join for working in rnds; rnds start at back of heel.

Next (dec) rnd: Needle 1, knit to last 3 sts, k2tog, k1; Needles 2 and 3, knit; Needle 4, k1, ssk, knit to end of rnd—2 sts dec'd.

Next rnd: Knit.

Rep last 2 rnds 7 more times—64 sts rem; 16 sts on each needle.

Foot

Work Rows 1–42 of Foot chart over 30 instep sts, working motifs using Intarsia in the Round technique (see Techniques).

With A, knit 1 rnd even.

Foot should measure about 7¼" (18.5 cm) from heel.

Shape Toe

Next (dec) rnd: Knit to last 2 sts of Needle 1, s2kp over last 2 sts of Needle 1 and first st of Needle 2; knit to end of rnd—2 st dec'd.

Rep last rnd 7 more times, shifting sts from Needle 4 to Needle 1, and from Needle 3 to Needle 2 as needed—14 sts dec'd.

Next (dec) rnd: Knit to last 2 sts of Needle 1, s2kp over last 2 sts of Needle 1 and first st of Needle 2; knit to last 2 sts of Needle 3, s2kp over last 2 sts of Needle 3 and first st of Needle 4; knit to end of rnd—4 sts dec'd.

Rep last rnd 7 more times—16 sts rem.

Next (dec) rnd: *K2tog; rep from * around—8 sts rem.

Cut yarn, leaving an 8" (20.5 cm) tail, thread tail through rem sts, pull tight to close hole, and fasten off on WS.

Left Sock

Work left sock same as right sock to heel.

Heel

Next row (RS): K16, turn.

Next row: Sl 1, p31, turn. Place rem 30 sts onto one needle or waste yarn for instep.

Work back and forth on rem 32 sts for heel.

Work Rows 1–32 of Left Heel chart.

Cont same as right sock to toe.

Shape Toe

Next (dec) rnd: Knit to last 2 sts of Needle 3, s2kp over last 2 sts of Needle 3 and first st of Needle 4; knit to end of rnd—2 st dec'd.

Rep last rnd 7 more times, shifting sts from Needle 1 to Needle 4, and from Needle 2 to Needle 3 as needed—14 sts dec'd.

Next (dec) rnd: Knit to last 2 sts of Needle 1, s2kp over last 2 sts of Needle 1 and first st of Needle 2; knit to last 2 sts of Needle 3, s2kp over last 2 sts of Needle 3 and first st of Needle 4; knit to end of rnd—4 sts dec'd.

Rep last rnd 7 more times—16 sts rem.

Next (dec) rnd: *K2tog; rep from * around—8 sts rem.

Cut yarn, leaving an 8" (20.5 cm) tail, thread tail through rem sts, pull tight to close hole, and fasten off on WS.

Finishing

Weave in ends.

Embroider socks foll charts.

Braid long tails.

Handwash in warm soapy water, carefully roll up in a towel, and gently squeeze out excess water. Reshape and leave to dry flat away from direct sun or heat source.

Press very lightly with a warm iron over a damp cloth.

LEFT HEEL

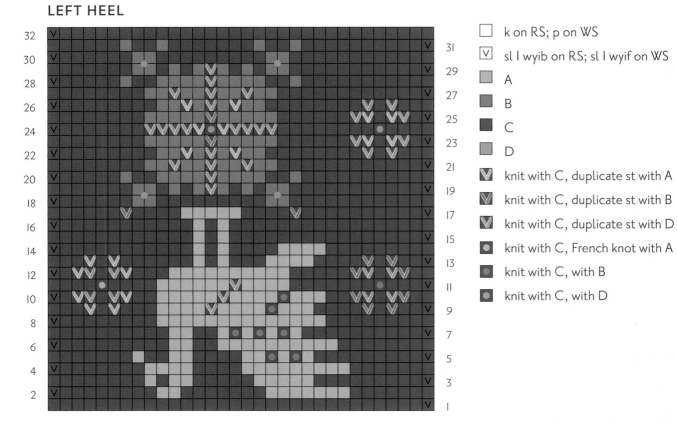

32 sts

RIGHT HEEL

32 sts

□ k on RS; p on WS

V̄ sl I wyib on RS; sl I wyif on WS

▨ A

▨ B

■ C

▨ D

V̈ knit with C, duplicate st with A

V̈ knit with C, duplicate st with B

V̈ knit with C, duplicate st with D

● knit with C, French knot with A

● knit with C, with B

● knit with C, with D

Lyyli Project Bag

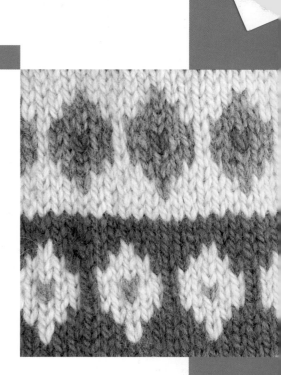

WHILE RUMMAGING in a secondhand bookstore in Helsinki I was lucky enough to find an original 1933 copy of *Kodin Neuletöitä*, a lovely little book filled with patterns for classic Finnish socks and mittens. A pair of traditional socks with a lovely decorative twined knitted border served as inspiration for the Lyyli Project Bag.

Knitted in a beautiful pure wool yarn, Lyyli is a quick and easy project to make. The simplicity of the two-color stranded colorwork and twined crook stitch detail pattern at the top of the bag makes it a perfect introduction to these classic Nordic knitting techniques. "Pockets," or simple bags with short handles, were used traditionally to carry knitting around in—the pocket was held over one arm and the knitter could move around still knitting. Knitted in the round with a simple linen lining, the Lyyli Project Bag makes an ideal contemporary knitting or project bag.

FINISHED MEASUREMENTS
About 14½" (37 cm) deep and 12" (30.5 cm) wide, washed.

YARN
Chunky weight (#5 Bulky).

Shown here: Hillesvåg Ullvarefabrikk AS Hifa Trollgarn (100% wool; 124 yd [114 m]/100 g): #728 Dark Green (A), 2 skeins; #737 Cream (B), I skein; #7040 Marled Green (C); I skein.

NEEDLES
Size U.S. 9 (5.5 mm) 24" (60 cm) circular (cir) and set of 4 double-pointed (dpn).

Adjust needle size if necessary to obtain the correct gauge.

NOTIONS
Marker (m); ¾ yd (68.5 cm) of lining fabric; matching thread and sewing needle; tapestry needle.

GAUGE
17 sts and 18 rnds = 4" (10 cm) over Body chart patt, after washing.

stitch guide

CROOK STITCH

The twined crook stitch here is worked over 3 stitches as P1,K1,P1 — with one strand held in front of work to purl with and one strand in back to knit with. Bring front strand in back to resume twined knitting.

It needs to be emphasized that the crook stitch here (used for the pattern specific to the Lyyli bag) is worked in this way, as crook stitches can also be worked K1,P1,K1.

Bag

With cir needle and A, CO 102 sts using Twined Cast-On (see Techniques). Place marker (pm) for beg of rnd and join for working in rnds.

RND 1: Work 1 rnd of twined purling (see Techniques).

RND 2: Work 1 rnd of twined knitting (see Techniques).

RND 3: Knit.

Work Rnds 1–22 of Body chart twice, then Rnds 1–11 once more. Cont with A only.

Work 1 rnd in twined knitting.

Work 1 rnd in twined purling.

Work 1 rnd in twined knitting.

Work Rnds 1–7 of Border chart in twined knitting and purling.

Work 1 rnd in twined knitting.

Work 1 rnd in twined purling.

Work 8 rnds in twined knitting.

Cut one strand of A. Join one strand of C. BO, continuing to twist the yarns as per twined knitting.

Handles (make 2)

With dpn and A, CO 8 sts. Arrange sts over 3 dpn. Pm for beg of rnd and join for working in rnds.

Work in St st until piece measures about 11¾" (30 cm) or desired length.

BO all sts.

Finishing

With A and C, duplicate st foll chart.

Arrange piece with beg/end of rnds at center back, sew bottom edge; make sure to sew through the back of each braided CO st so the braided CO edge remains visible at edge.

Weave in ends.

Handwash in warm soapy water, very carefully roll up in a towel, and gently squeeze out excess water. Reshape and leave to dry away from direct sun or heat source. On WS press very lightly with a warm iron over a damp cloth.

Using the finished bag as a template, cut lining fabric to fit. With matching thread and sewing needle, sew side and bottom edges. Place lining into bag, with WS of lining to WS of bag.

Fold top edge of bag to WS and over top edge of the lining. Sew top edge of bag in place.

Using the finished handles as a template, cut 2 pieces of lining fabric the same length as the handles. Fold them lengthwise into tubes. With matching thread and sewing needle, sew side edges together. Insert lining pieces into the handles without stretching handles. Pin handles to WS of bag, placing CO and BO edges at BO edge of bag. Sew handles to bag along all edges, including top edge of bag.

	A
☒	A
☐	B
⊡	C
⩔	k with B, duplicate st with C
⩔	k with C, duplicate st with A
☐	knit
‿•	crook st (see Stitch Guide)
☐	pattern repeat

COLOR

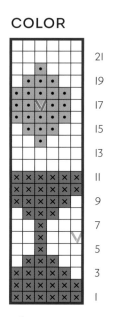

6-st repeat

BORDER

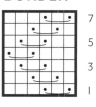

6-st repeat

kettu top

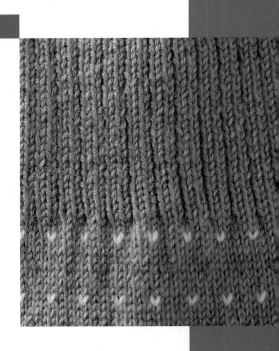

KETTU IS the Finnish word for "fox," and there is a very special Finnish myth that explains how an Arctic fox was apparently responsible for creating the ethereal aurora borealis, otherwise known as the northern lights. This busy fox started fires as it ran about on the snow, sweeping up the snow and ice crystals with his bushy tail and scattering them far and wide like embers and sparks into the night sky. However, the foxes on the Kettu Top look more like they are quietly contemplating an ice flower that has suddenly appeared during a magical snowstorm!

This little Kettu top is knitted in the round but split at the armholes. The ribbed top part is then knitted backward and forward on two needles. Duplicate stitch is used to fill in the lice stitch pattern, and simple embroidery stitches are made for the fox's eyes, nose, whiskers, paws, and snowflake patterning. A single row of twined knitting around the neck and armholes creates a subtle decorative edge

FINISHED MEASUREMENTS
27" (68.5 cm) chest circumference and 13¾" (35 cm) long.

YARN
Sport weight (#2 Fine).

Shown here: Dale Garn Heilo (100% Norwegian wool; 109 yd [100 m]/1¾ oz [50 g]): #6642 Light Steel Blue (A), 4 balls; #3237 Orange Red (B), I ball; #0020 Natural (C), I ball; #5762 Steel Grey (D), small amount for embroidery.

NEEDLES
Size 3 mm (no equivalent; between U.S. sizes 2 and 3) 24" (60 cm) circular (cir) and 2 double-pointed (dpn).

Adjust needle size if necessary to obtain the correct gauge.

Size U.S. 2 (2.75 mm) 16" (40.5 cm) circular (cir) and set of 5 double-pointed (dpn).

CROCHET HOOK
Size 2.5 mm (no equivalent; between U.S. sizes B-I and C-2).

NOTIONS
Markers (m); holders or waste yarn; tapestry needle.

GAUGE
25½ sts and 31 rnds = 4" (10 cm) in lice st patt on larger needles; 28 sts and 33 rnds in rib patt on larger needles, after washing.

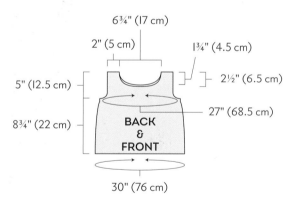

6¾" (17 cm)

2" (5 cm)

1¾" (4.5 cm)

2½" (6.5 cm)

5" (12.5 cm)

8¾" (22 cm)

27" (68.5 cm)

BACK & FRONT

30" (76 cm)

Body

With larger cir needle and A, CO 192 sts using Knitted Cast-On (see Techniques). Place marker (pm) and join for working in rnds.

Rnds 1–3: *K2, p1; rep from * to end of rnd.

Rnd 4: Join B and work in established rib.

Rnd 5: Join C and work in established rib. Cut C.

Rnd 6: With B, work in established rib. Cut B.

Rnds 7–9: With A, work in established rib.

Next (dec) rnd: Ssk, knit to last 2 sts, ssk—190 sts.

Next rnd: Work 95 sts in Row 1 of chart, pm, work 95 sts in Row 1 of chart.

Work Rows 2–30 of chart as established, then rep Rows 23–30 three more times.

With A, knit 3 rnds even. Piece should measure 8¼" (21 cm) from beg.

Next (dec) rnd: *Ssk, k1, p1, (k2, p1) to 4 sts before m, ssk, k1, p1; rep from * once more—186 sts rem (93 sts each for front and back).

Work 3 rnds in K2, P1 rib.

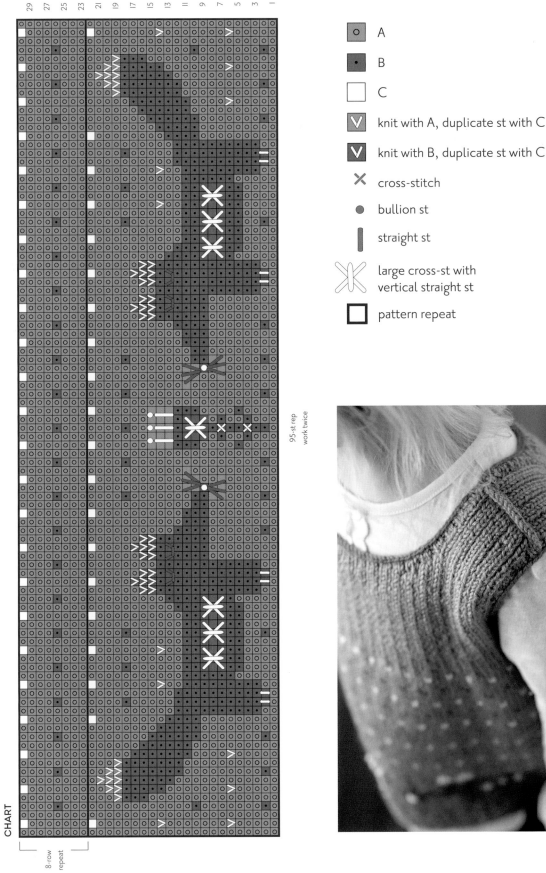

8-row repeat

95-st rep
work twice

○ A

· B

□ C

V knit with A, duplicate st with C

V knit with B, duplicate st with C

✕ cross-stitch

● bullion st

| straight st

large cross-st with vertical straight st

□ pattern repeat

Front

NEXT RND: BO 2 sts, work in established patt to marker, place rem 93 sts on holder or waste yarn for back—91 sts rem for front. Cont working back and forth.

BO 2 sts at the beg of next 7 rows, then 1 st at beg of next 2 rows—75 sts rem.

Cont even until piece measures 11¼" (28.5 cm) from beg, ending with a WS row.

Shape Neck

NEXT ROW (RS): Work 21 sts, place next 33 sts on holder or waste yarn for front neck, join a second ball of yarn, and work to end—21 sts rem each side.

BO at each neck edge 2 sts twice, then 1 st 3 times—14 sts rem each side.

Cont even until piece measures 13¾" (35 cm) from beg. Place rem shoulder sts on holders or waste yarn.

Back

Shape armholes same as front—75 sts.

Cont even until piece measures 12" (30.5 cm) from beg, ending with a WS row.

Shape Neck

NEXT ROW (RS): Work 24 sts, place next 27 sts on holder or waste yarn for back neck, join a second ball of yarn, and work to end—24 sts rem each side.

BO at each neck edge 4 sts twice, then 2 sts once—14 sts rem each side.

Cont even until piece measures 13¾" (35 cm) from beg.

Return held front shoulder sts to dpn. Hold front and back with WS tog and RS facing. Join shoulders using Three-Needle BO on RS.

Neck Edge

With smaller cir needle, A and with RS facing, beg at left shoulder, pick up and knit I st in seam, 20 sts along left front neck, work held 33 front neck sts in established rib, pick up and knit 39 sts along right neck edge, work held 27 back neck sts in established rib, then pick up and knit 18 sts along left back neck edge—138 sts. Pm and join for working in rnds.

RND 1: KI, pl, (k2, pl) to last st, kI.

RND 2: Change to B and work in established rib.

RND 3: Working in twined knitting (see Techniques), BO all sts.

Armhole Edges (work both the same)

With dpn, A and RS facing, beg at bottom of armhole, pick up and knit 63 sts evenly along edge. Pm and join for working in rnds.

RND 1: *K2, pl; rep from * to end of rnd.

RND 2: Change to B and work in established rib.

RND 3: Working in twined knitting, BO all sts.

Finishing

With crochet hook, A and RS facing, work I rnd of single crochet along bottom edge. Fasten off.

Embroider lower body foll chart.

Weave in ends.

Handwash in warm soapy water, very carefully roll up in a towel, and gently squeeze out excess water. Reshape and leave to dry flat away from direct sun or heat source. On WS, press very lightly with a warm iron over a damp cloth.

matti gloves

T HESE GLOVES are a great example of how an
unmistakably Nordic-looking design can be achieved
by combining traditional knitting techniques from various
Northern countries. Traditional Fair Isle patterns and a Shetland
color palette are complemented with a colorful Estonian
braided cast-on and a patterned rib. A three-color band of
Estonian nuppid (or knotted) relief stitches decorate the wrist,
and duplicate stitches and French knots are worked in gold and
bright blue to further embellish the Fair Isle motifs on the front
of the gloves. To help you distinguish between the front and
back (palms) of the gloves, which are both knitted with the same
geometric patterns, only the fronts have been embroidered.

The Matti gloves have been designed to be practical working
gloves and have a well-shaped thumb gusset and individual
forchettes between each of the fingers to allow ease of
movement. You could also increase the warmth factor by
wearing these gloves over the top of a much finer pair.

FINISHED MEASUREMENTS
9½" (24 cm) hand circumference
and 11½" (29 cm) long.

YARN
Fingering weight (#1 Super Fine).

Shown here: Jamieson's of
Shetland Spindrift (100% wool;
115 yd [105 m]/25 g): #1020
Nighthawk (A), 2 skeins; #127
Pebble (B), I skein; #462 Ginger
(C), I skein; #75 Turquoise (D), I
skein; #126 Charcoal (E), I skein;
#123 Oxford (F), I skein; #680
Lunar (G), I skein; #289 Gold (H),
small amount for embroidery.

NEEDLES
Set of 5 size U.S. 2 (2.75 mm)
double-pointed (dpn).

*Adjust needle size if necessary to
obtain the correct gauge.*

NOTIONS
Markers (m); waste yarn or
holder; tapestry needle.

GAUGE
35 sts and 35 rnds = 4" (10 cm)
in chart patt, after washing.

Right Glove

With A and B, CO 69 sts using the Two-Color Fishtail Cast-On (see Techniques) with A on right needle and B on left needle; do not include slipknot in stitch total. Sl last st on right needle to left needle.

Next (dec) rnd: With A, k2tog tbl, then knit tbl around—69 sts. Distribute sts evenly over 4 dpn. Place marker (pm) and join for working in rnds.

Next (dec) rnd: P2tog, purl to end of rnd—68 sts (17 sts on each needle).

Rib

Rnds 1–4: *K2 A, p2 E; rep from * to end of rnd.

Rnds 5–8: *K2 A, p2 F; rep from * to end of rnd.

Rnds 9 and 10: *K2 A, p2 B; rep from * to end of rnd.

Rnd 11: *K2 A, p2 C; rep from * to end of rnd.

Rnd 12: *K2 A, p2 B; rep from * to end of rnd.

Rnd 13: *K2 A, p2 C; rep from * to end of rnd.

Rnds 14 and 15: *K2 A, p2 B; rep from * to end of rnd.

Rnds 16–19: *K2 A, p2 F; rep from * to end of rnd.

Rnds 20–23: *K2 A, p2 E; rep from * to end of rnd.

Next (inc) rnd: With A only, *k1, MI, knit to last st on needle, MI, k1; rep from * to end of rnd—76 sts (19 sts on each needle).

Next rnd: Keeping unused yarns at back of work, *k1 A, k1 B, k1 C; rep from * to end of rnd.

Next rnd: Keeping unused yarns at back of work, *p1 A, p1 B, p1 C; rep from * to end of rnd.

Next rnd: With E, knit.

Work Rnds 1–5 of Hand chart.

Rnd 6 (inc): With F, (knit to end of needle, MI) 4 times—80 sts.

Thumb Gusset

Rnd 7: MIR B, pm, work next rnd of Hand chart to end, pm, MIL B.

Cont from Rnd 2 of Thumb chart, and work as established through Rnd 29 of Hand chart, and Rnd 23 of Thumb chart—102 sts (80 sts for hand, and 22 sts for thumb).

Rnd 30: Place 22 thumb sts on waste yarn or holder, using backward loop method (see Techniques), CO 3 sts, work Rnd 30 of Hand chart to end of rnd, CO 4 sts over gap, pm—87 sts.

Work Rnds 31–41 of Hand chart—81 sts rem.

☐ knit	◤ A
☑ k2tog	☐ B
☑ ssk	☒ C
☑ sk2p	◮ E
MR make I right	⊙ G
ML make I left	● knit with G, French knot with G
☐ pattern repeat	⊻ knit with B, duplicate st with A
	⊻ knit with B, duplicate st with D
	⊻ knit with G, duplicate st with H
	⊻ knit with E, duplicate st with C

HAND

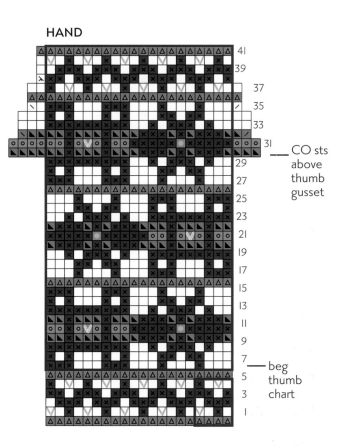

—— CO sts above thumb gusset

—— beg thumb chart

THUMB

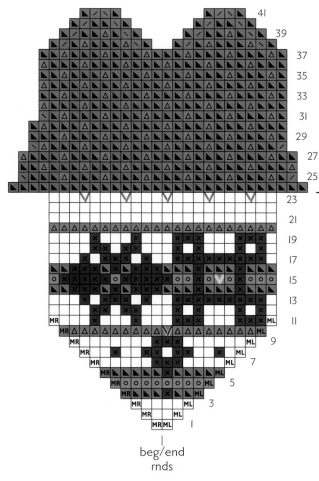

—— pick up sts in CO edge at top of thumb opening; beg rnds at center of picked up sts.

beg/end rnds

INDEX, MIDDLE, AND RING FINGERS

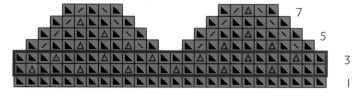

26 sts

☑ k2tog	◼ A
☒ ssk	◼ E

Index Finger

With A, k9, k1f&b, place next 60 sts on waste yarn or holder, use backward-loop method to CO 3 sts, k1f&b, k10—26 sts. Divide sts with 7 sts each on Needles 1 and 3, and 6 sts each on Needles 2 and 4. Pm and join for working in rnds. Beg rnds at front (back of hand).

Work Rnds 2 and 3 of Finger chart until finger measures about ½" (1.3 cm) short of desired length, ending with Rnd 3.

Shape Top

Work Rnds 4–7 of Finger chart—10 sts rem.

Cut yarn, leaving an 8" (20.5 cm) tail, thread tail through rem sts, pull tight to close hole, and fasten off on WS.

Middle Finger

Place first 10 sts and last 10 sts onto dpn, leave rem 40 sts on holders. Join A, pick up and knit 3 sts in CO sts at base of index finger, k10, CO 3 sts, k10—26 sts. Pm and join for working in rnds.

Work middle finger same as index finger.

Ring Finger

Place first 10 sts and last 10 sts onto dpn, leave rem 20 sts on holders. Join A, pick up and knit 3 sts in CO sts at base of middle finger, k10, CO 3 sts, k10—26 sts. Pm and join for working in rnds.

Work ring finger same as index finger.

Little Finger

Place rem 20 sts onto dpn. Join A, pick up and knit 3 sts in CO sts at base of ring finger—23 sts. Pm and join for working in rnds.

Next (inc) rnd: Knit to last 2 sts, k1f&b, k1—24 sts.

Work Rnds 2 and 3 of Little Finger chart until finger measures about ½" (1.3 cm) short of desired length, ending with Rnd 3.

LITTLE FINGER

7

5

3

1

24 sts

Shape Top

Work Rnds 4–7 of Little Finger chart—8 sts rem.

Cut yarn, leaving an 8" (20.5 cm) tail, thread tail through rem sts, pull tight to close hole, and fasten off on WS.

Left Glove

Work left glove same as right glove.

Finishing

Weave in ends.

Embroider thumb and back of each hand only foll charts.

Handwash in warm soapy water, carefully roll up in a towel, and gently squeeze out excess water. Reshape and leave to dry flat away from direct sun or heat source.

On WS, press very lightly with a warm iron over a damp cloth.

stig sprig cushion

THE ROWS of stylized flowers and leafy sprigs that pattern this cushion were inspired by the wonderfully colorful, and often humorous, ceramics and textiles designed in the 1950s and 1960s by Swedish artist Stig Lindberg. The Stig Sprig Cushion is knitted in the round, and the repetitive nature of the design makes it easy to follow and quick to work. It has a provisional cast-on that is later joined with a three-needle bind-off, and a two-stitch I-cord as a buttonband. Simple embroidery stitches are used to embellish the flowers.

Traditionally, brightly colored, decorative, flat cushions such as the Stig Sprig Cushion were used on chairs, long benches, and in sleighs throughout Scandinavia. I would recommend making your own cushion pad for the Stig Sprig—all you will need to do is cut a piece of linen to the size required, sew up all but a small section of the seams, fill it with pure wool, and sew the remaining seam closed.

FINISHED MEASUREMENTS
21½" (54.5 cm) wide and 15" (38 cm) long.

YARN
Sportweight (#2 Fine).

Shown here: Dale Garn Heilo (100% Norwegian wool; 109 yd [100 m]/1¾ oz [50 g]): #0090 Black (A), 6 balls; #9145 Asparagus (B), 2 balls; #7062 Petrol (C), 1 ball; #6642 Light Steel Blue (D), 1 ball.

NEEDLES
Size 3 mm (no equivalent; between U.S. sizes 2 and 3) circular (cir) and 2 double-pointed (dpn).

Adjust needle size if necessary to obtain the correct gauge.

NOTIONS
Marker (m); ½ yd (45.5 cm) lining fabric; sewing needle and matching thread; fiberfill; six ⅝" (16 mm) buttons; tapestry needle.

GAUGE
25 sts and 28 rnds = 4" (10 cm) in chart patt, after washing.

NOTE
Use 2 strands of yarn when working the 10 rnds in black, using them just as if you were knitting a Fair Isle/stranded pattern as follows: *k4 with first strand, k1 with second strand; rep from * on back, and *k2 with first strand, p2 with second strand; rep from * on front rib and make sure to bring second strand to WS before knitting the next 2 sts. There should be a consistent thickness to the one-color areas so that they are the same as the color-patterned area.

FLOWER

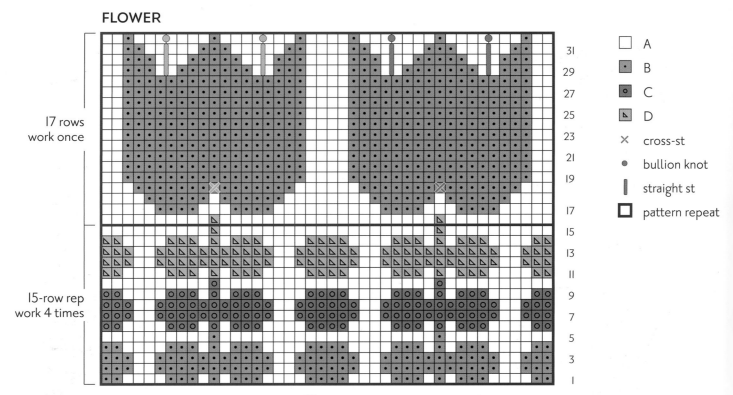

17 rows work once

15-row rep work 4 times

31
29
27
25
23
21
19
17
15
13
11
9
7
5
3
1

Legend:
- ☐ A
- ▣ B
- ▣ C
- ◹ D
- ✕ cross-st
- ● bullion knot
- | straight st
- ☐ pattern repeat

42-st rep work 7 times

- -

Cushion

With A and cir needle, CO 294 sts using a provisional method (see Techniques). Place marker (pm) and join for working in rnds.

Join a second strand of A.

RNDS 1–10: Knit (see Note).

Work Rnds 1–15 of chart 4 times, then work Rnds 16–32 once.

Cut B.

Join second strand of A, knit 8 rnds.

Cont with both strands of A as foll:

NEXT (DEC) RND: Ssk, k145, ssk, k1, (p2, k2) to end of rnd—292 sts rem.

NEXT RND: K146; (k2, p2) to last 2 sts, k2.

Rep last rnd 8 more times.

NEXT RND: K146, BO rem 146 sts—146 sts rem.

NEXT ROW (RS): (K2, p2) to last 2 sts, k2.

NEXT ROW: (P2, k2) to last 2 sts, p2.

Rep last 2 rows 8 more times. Cut one strand of A.

BO all sts kwise.

Remove provisional CO and place sts onto cir needle—294 sts. With RS facing, divide sts with 147 sts on each half of needle. Join A at beg/end of rnds. Join bottom edge using Three-Needle BO.

Finishing

Weave in ends.

Embroider cushion foll chart.

I-Cord

With A and dpn, CO 2 sts.

Row 1: K2, slide sts back to right end of dpn.

Row 2: Bring yarn cross back and k2, slide sts back to right end of dpn.

Rep Row 2 until I-cord is same length as front BO edge.

BO.

Sew I-cord to front BO edge, leaving 6 openings, each 4 sts wide, for buttonholes between each flower.

Fold front ribbed border over back ribbed border. Sew side edges of front border to back.

Handwash in warm soapy water, very carefully roll up in a towel, and gently squeeze out excess water. Reshape and leave to dry flat away from direct sun or heat source.

On WS, press very lightly using a warm iron over a damp cloth.

Using finished cushion as a template, cut 2 pieces of lining fabric for insert. Sew 3 sides of lining, and most of 4th side. Turn insert with RS facing and fill with pure wool, sew rem opening closed.

Sew buttons to back below ribbed border under buttonholes. Place insert inside cushion.

ole Reindeer mittens

TRADITIONAL KNITTING techniques from several different Northern countries have been combined to create an unmistakably Nordic-looking pair of cozy little mittens. The reindeer motif is a very old and sacred Nordic symbol, and images of stylized reindeer and other antlered animals have been found in ancient cave paintings and stone carvings throughout Scandinavia. The stylized reindeer pattern is synonymous specifically with the stylized black-and-white motifs of traditional Norwegian Selbu knitting. These sacred reindeer shapes would often be accompanied by a small geometric stylized sun symbol, just as they are here.

The Ole Reindeer Mittens have been knitted in the round with 5 double-pointed needles in a fingering-weight, pure Shetland wool and have a two-color Estonian braided cast-on and traditional Norwegian patterns. These patterns and the reindeer are decorated with simple duplicate stitches and embroidery stitches and, once completed, the mittens are washed in warm soapy water and left to dry flat.

FINISHED MEASUREMENTS
6" (15 cm) hand circumference and 6" (15 cm) long.

YARN
Fingering weight (#1 Super Fine).

Shown here: Jamieson's of Shetland Spindrift (100% wool; 115 yd [105 m]/25 g): #680 Lunar (A), I skein; #304 White (B), I skein; #462 Ginger (C), very small amount for the cast-on and embroidery; #289 Gold (D), very small amount for embroidery.

NEEDLES
Set of 5 size U.S. 2 (2.75 mm) double-pointed (dpn).

Adjust needle size if necessary to obtain the correct gauge.

NOTIONS
Marker (m); holder or waste yarn; tapestry needle.

GAUGE
31 sts and 36 rnds = 4" (10 cm) in chart patt in the round after washing.

Right Mitten

With B and C, and dpn, CO 45 sts using Two-Color Fishtail Cast-On method (see Techniques) with B on left needle and C on right needle; do not include slip-knot in stitch total. Divide sts evenly over 4 dpn. Join using Crossover Join (see Techniques). Cut yarns. Place marker (pm) and join for working in rnds.

Next rnd: With A, k2tog tbl, knit tbl to last 2 sts, k2tog tbl—44 sts. Adjust sts if necessary with 11 sts on each needle.

Next rnd: *K2, p2; rep from * around.

Rep last rnd 17 more times.

Next (inc) rnd: Needle 1, join B, M1 B, start at st 2 of Right Hand chart and work Rnd 1 to end of Needle 2; Needle 3, M1 A, cont from st 25 of chart, work to end of rnd—46 sts. Arrange sts with 12 sts each on Needles 1 and 2, and 11 sts each on Needles 3 and 4.

Work Rnds 2–10 of chart.

Rnd 11: Needles 1, 2, and 3, work as established to last 10 sts, place next 9 sts on holder or waste yarn, using both colors and backward-loop method (see Techniques), CO 9 sts above gap, alternating colors for each st, work to end of rnd.

Cont through Rnd 39—10 sts rem.

Cut yarns, leaving an 8" (20.5 cm) tail, thread tail through rem sts, pull tight to close hole, and fasten off on WS.

Thumb

Return 9 held sts to dpn, pick up and knit 9 sts along the CO sts above the opening foll colors in Thumb chart—18 sts. Distribute sts with 5 sts each on Needles 1 and 3, and 4 sts each on Needles 2 and 4. Pm and join for working in rnds.

Work Rnds 1–12 of Thumb chart—10 sts rem.

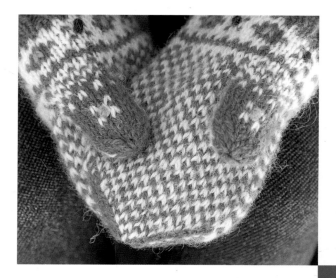

Cut yarns, leaving an 8" (20.5 cm) tail, thread tail through rem sts, pull tight to close hole, and fasten off on WS.

Left Mitten

Work left mitten same as right mitten through Rnd 10.

Rnd 11: Work 2 sts as established, place next 9 sts on holder or waste yarn, using both colors and backward loop method, CO 9 sts above gap, alternating colors for each st, work to end of rnd.

Cont same as right mitten.

Finishing

Weave in ends.

Embroider mittens foll charts.

Handwash in warm soapy water, carefully roll up in a towel, and gently squeeze out excess water. Reshape and leave to dry flat away from direct sun or heat source.

On WS, press very lightly with a warm iron over a damp cloth.

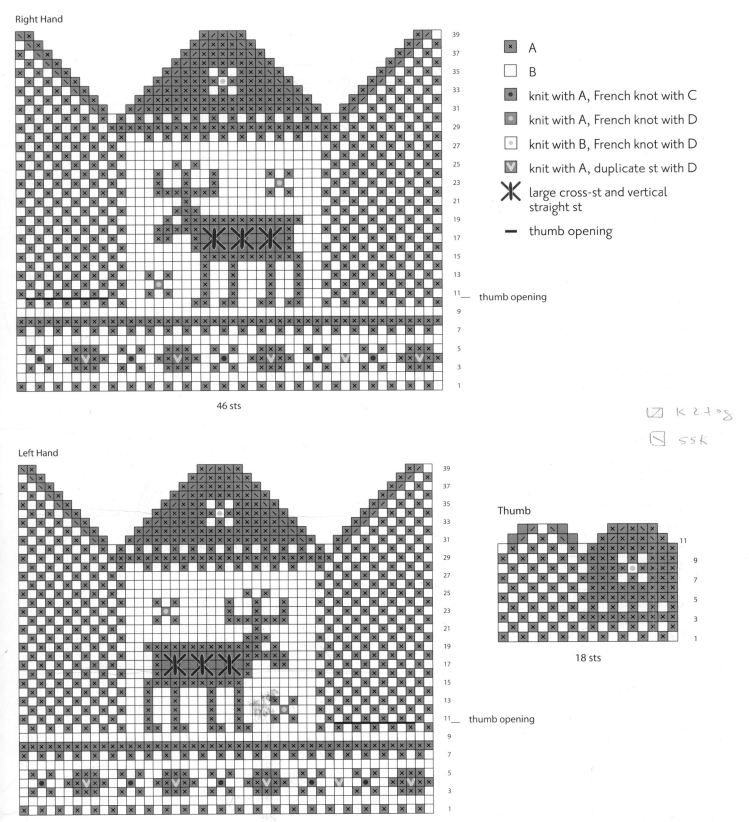

Right Hand

Left Hand

Thumb

46 sts

46 sts

18 sts

	A
☒	A
☐	B
●	knit with A, French knot with C
◉	knit with A, French knot with D
⊙	knit with B, French knot with D
V	knit with A, duplicate st with D
✕	large cross-st and vertical straight st
—	thumb opening

thumb opening

thumb opening

elfur socks

THESE BEAUTIFULLY colorful and patterned little Elfur Socks were inspired by the traditional fantastically colored and patterned knitted stockings made on the Estonian island of Muhu. The Elfur Socks are knitted from the top down and have a colored rib pattern, a small plaited tassel, traditional geometric patterns on the leg, and bands of colorful patterns on the foot. French knots and duplicate stitches are used to further embellish the designs. The Elfur Socks have a traditional Estonian heel, which is worked after the rest of the sock has been completed, as well as a distinctive Estonian toe shaping. The shaping of both the heel and toe is done with a specific Estonian decrease technique.

Not only will the Elfur Socks be wonderful to wear, but they would also look very sweet hung up and filled with little festive treats. You could make a larger pair of Elfur Socks by using a heavier weight of yarn—you just need to follow the suggested gauge of whichever yarn you substitute.

FINISHED MEASUREMENTS

6½" (16.5 cm) foot circumference and 6" (15 cm) long.

YARN

Sock weight (#1 Super Fine).

Shown here: Cascade Heritage Sock Yarn (75% superwash merino wool, 25% nylon; 437 yd [399 m]/100 g): #5646 Pumpkin (A), #5606 Burgundy (B), #5612 Moss (C), #5628 Cotton Candy (D), 1 skein each.

NEEDLES

Set of 5 size U.S. 1 (2.25 mm) double-pointed (dpn).

Set of 5 size U.S. 2 (2.75 mm) double-pointed (dpn).

Adjust needle size if necessary to obtain the correct gauge.

NOTIONS

Marker (m); waste yarn; tapestry needle.

GAUGE

32 sts and 38½ rnds = 4" (10 cm) in chart patt using larger needles, after washing.

Rib

With C and smaller dpn, CO 54 sts using the Cable Cast-On method (see Techniques), leaving long tail for braided cord. Place marker (pm) and join for working in rnds.

RNDS 1–4: *K2, p1; rep from * around.

RND 5: Join A leaving a long tail for braided cord, *k1 A, (k1, p1) with C; rep from * around.

RND 6: With A, *k2, p1; rep from * around.

RND 7: Join D leaving a long tail for braided cord, *k2, p1; rep from * around. Cut D.

RND 8: With A, *k2, p1; rep from * around.

RND 9: *K1 A, (k1, p1) with C; rep from * around. Cut A.

RNDS 10–13: With C, *k2, p1; rep from * around.

Leg

Change to larger dpn.

NEXT (DEC) RND: With C, ssk, knit to end of rnd— 53 sts.

Knit 2 rnds even.

Work Rnds 1–31 of Leg chart.

NEXT RND: With C, knit.

NEXT (DEC) RND: Knit to last 2 sts, k2tog—52 sts.

Place Heel

Distribute sts if necessary with 13 sts on each needle.

NEXT 2 RNDS: Needles 1, 2 and 3, knit; Needles 4 and 1, with waste yarn, knit; return to Needle 4 and C, knit; Needles 1–4, knit.

Foot

Work Rnds 1–35 of Foot chart. Foot should measure about 3¾" (9.5 cm) from waste yarn from heel.

Toe

NEXT RND: With B, knit.

NEXT (DEC) RND: Knit to last 2 sts of Needle 1, work Muhu Dec (see Techniques) over last 2 sts of Needle 1 and first st of Needle 2, knit to last 2 sts of Needle 3, work Muhu Dec over last 2 sts of Needle 3 and first st of Needle 4, knit to end—4 sts dec'd.

Rep last rnd 10 more times—8 sts rem.

Cut yarn, leaving an 8" (20.5 cm) tail, thread tail through rem sts, pull tight to close hole, and fasten off on WS.

If you want to get the exact measurement of a child's foot, work the heel before starting the toe, then cont 35-rnd rep of Foot chart to about 1" (2.5 cm) short of desired length from heel.

Heel

Remove waste yarn from heel, and place 52 loops on 4 dpn with 13 sts on each needle—52 sts. Pm for beg of rnd and join for working in rnds; rnds beg at back of heel.

Next (dec) rnd: With A, knit to last 2 sts of Needle 1, work Muhu Dec over last 2 sts of Needle 1 and first st of Needle 2, knit to last 2 sts of Needle 3, work Muhu Dec over last 2 sts of Needle 3 and first st of Needle 4, knit to end—4 sts dec'd.

Rep last rnd 10 more times—8 sts rem.

Cut yarn, leaving an 8" (20.5 cm) tail, thread tail through rem sts, pull tight to close hole, and fasten off on WS.

Foot measures about 6" (15 cm) from heel to toe.

Finishing

Weave in ends.

Embroider socks foll chart.

Braid long tails.

Handwash in warm soapy water, carefully roll up in a towel, and gently squeeze out excess water. Reshape and leave to dry flat away from direct sunlight or heat source.

On WS, press very lightly with a warm iron over a damp cloth.

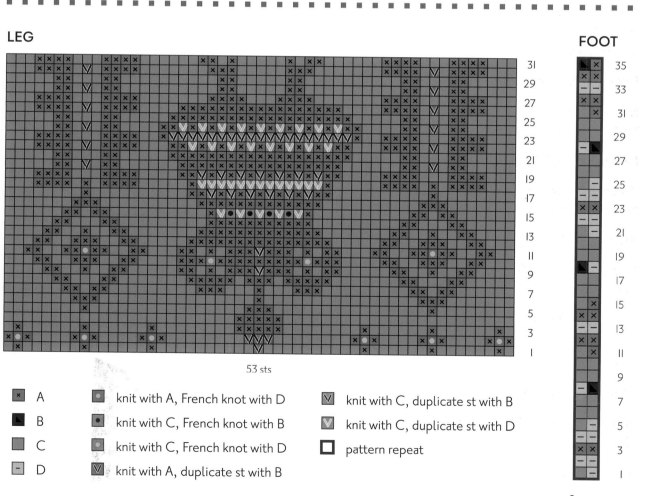

LEG

53 sts

FOOT

2-st rep

	A		knit with A, French knot with D		knit with C, duplicate st with B
	B		knit with C, French knot with B		knit with C, duplicate st with D
	C		knit with C, French knot with D		pattern repeat
	D		knit with A, duplicate st with B		

folk textures

Thrumming, a technique in which strands of either raw fleece or leftover woolen yarn from weaving or knitting are incorporated into the knitting, also creates a dense and superinsulated fabric. Thrums are incorporated into knitted fabric at regular intervals, either onto the outside to create a shaggy effect, into the back of the knitting to form part of the pattern, or invisibly into the inside just as insulation.

Although folk knitting is generally associated with allover geometric patterning in two or more contrasting colors, there is a more understated type of traditional knitting consisting of plain and textural areas that were often only knitted in one color.

Classic examples of textural folk knits include traditional fishermen's jerseys, or "ganseys," from England and Holland; cabled, bobbled, and twisted Irish Aran designs; Danish damask knitting; intricate twisted or traveling stitches found on Northern mittens and socks and the "deep" purl stitches; and crook stitches and crook paths, which are used to make the distinctive, nubby designs on twined knitting.

In the cold and harsh Northern climates, knitted items needed to be practical, warm, and reliable. So it is not at all surprising that the wonderfully warm, double-thick fabric that is created by tvåänststickat—"two-ended" or twined knitting—originated in Sweden. Fair Isle and stranded knitting techniques, which similarly yield a double-thick fabric, also originated in the North and Scandinavian countries.

English seamen's hats are some of the earliest surviving examples of knitted thrumming, and throughout Scandinavia and other Northern countries there was a tradition for decorative, colorfully thrummed mittens.

Embroidery and many woven designs were often copied to create not only geometric patterns but also textural knitted stitches. Decorative knitting techniques such as Estonian nupps and nuppiline (knotted) stitches, vikkel braids, knitted braided cast-ons, twisted or "traveling" stitches, and colorful fringing all evolved.

snorri cushion

T HE SNORRI Cushion was inspired by the lovely two-color allover geometric patterns and colorful braided borders found on traditional Estonian mittens. Plump and cozy, this cushion is knitted in the round with a decorative braided cast-on and twined stitch border details. The two-color stranded pattern, which is actually deceptively straightforward to knit, is embellished with a few simple duplicate stitches. Knitted in a chunky pure wool yarn, this is an easy project that will enable you to familiarize yourself with some classic Nordic mitten-making techniques. Traditionally Estonian mittens were made on very fine needles with an extremely dense stitch count, so this cushion is definitely an easier and quicker project to get started on!

I would recommend making your own cushion pad to go inside the Snorri Cushion. You will just need to cut a piece of linen to the size required, sew up all but a small section of the seams, fill it with pure wool, and sew closed the remaining seam.

FINISHED MEASUREMENTS
18" (45.5 cm) wide and 14½" (37 cm) long.

YARN
Chunky weight (#5 Bulky).

Shown here: Hillesvåg Ullvarefabrikk AS Hifa Trollgarn (100% wool; 124 yd [114 m]/3½ oz [100 g]): #704 Mid Grey (A),
2 skeins; #702 Natural (B), 2 skeins; #703 Light Grey (C), 1 skein; #719 Berry Red (D), 1 skein.

NEEDLES
Size U.S. 9 (5.5 mm) 32" (80 cm) circular (cir).

Adjust needle size if necessary to obtain the correct gauge.

NOTIONS
Marker (m); ½ yd (45.5 cm) lining fabric; sewing needle and matching thread; pure wool for filling; tapestry needle.

GAUGE
17 sts and 19 rnds = 4" (10 cm) in chart patt after washing.

Cushion

Border

With C and D, and cir needle use Two-Color Fishtail Cast-On (see Techniques) with C on left needle and D on right needle, CO 161 sts; do not include slipknot in stitch total.

Next (dec) rnd (RS): Work in twined purling, p2tog D, *p1 C, p1 D; rep, from * to 1 st before slipknot, p2tog C—160 sts. Join using Crossover Join (see Techniques). Place marker (pm).

Cut D.

Next rnd: Join B, knit.

Cut C.

Next rnd: Join A, knit.

Motif

Work chart Rnds 1–16 four times, then work Rnd 17 once.

Next rnd: With A, knit.

Next rnd: With B, knit.

Cut B.

Border

Next rnd: Join D, *k1 D, k1 A; rep from * around.

Cut A.

Next rnd: Work in twined purling, *p1 D, p1 C; rep from * around.

Next rnd: BO as you go, work in twined knitting as foll: *k1 tbl D, k1 tbl C; rep from * around.

 A

□ B

Ⅴ knit with A, duplicate st with D

□ pattern repeat

CHART

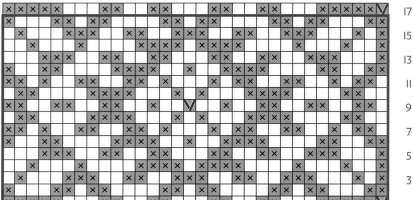

32-st rep

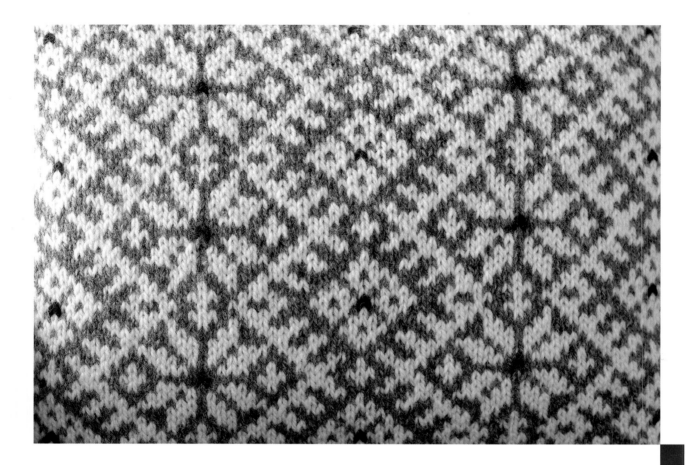

Finishing

Weave in ends.

Embroider cushion foll chart.

Handwash in warm soapy water, very carefully roll up in a towel, and gently squeeze out excess water. Reshape and leave to dry flat away from direct sun or heat source.

On WS, press very lightly using a warm iron over a damp cloth.

Arrange piece with beg/end of rnds at center back, sew bottom edge; make sure to sew through the back of each braided CO st so the braided CO edge remains visible at edge.

Using finished cushion as a template, cut 2 pieces of lining fabric for insert. Sew 3 sides and most of 4th side. Turn insert with RS facing and fill with pure wool. Sew rem opening closed. Place insert inside cushion and sew top edge of cushion; make sure to sew through the back of each twined BO st so the braided edge remains visible at edge.

emmi yoked top

S IMPLE WHITE or natural linen peasant blouses were the inspiration for this little top. These traditional blouses were often elaborately gathered at the neck and shoulders and were often beautifully embroidered in either bright, colorful designs or in gorgeous, textural relief patterns in natural tones. Knitted in the round from the bottom up, the yoke on the Emmi Yoked Top echoes these gathered effects. Simple traveling, or twisted, stitches usually found as decorative bands or detailing on mittens and socks have been used as features at the waist and on the back. These stitches also help give a gathered effect to the top. The hem, which is knitted deep and folded over, also has a small twisted-stitch detail. This not only adds a subtle pattern but also is a helpful guide for folding and stitching the hem. Knitted in pure wool on a circular needle, this top is washed in warm soapy water and left to dry flat on completion.

FINISHED MEASUREMENTS
38" (96.5 cm) bust circumference and 19¼" (49 cm) long at center of back.

YARN
Worsted weight (#4 Medium).

Shown here: LB Collection Organic Wool (100% organic wool; 185 yd [170 m]/3½ oz [100 g]): Natural, 5 skeins.

NEEDLES
Size U.S. 7 (4.5 mm) 40" (100 cm) circular (cir) and set of 5 double-pointed (dpn).

Adjust needle size if necessary to obtain the correct gauge.

NOTIONS
Marker (m); cable needle (cn); holders or waste yarn; tapestry needle.

GAUGE
17 sts and 27 rnds = 4" (10 cm) in St st after washing.

stitch guide

RC (1 over 1 Right Cross): Sl 1 st to cn and hold in back, k1 tbl from left needle, k1 tbl from cn.

LC (1 over 1 Left Cross): Sl 1 st to cn and hold in front, k1 tbl from left needle, k1 tbl from cn.

RT (1K over 1P Right Cross): Sl 1 st to cn and hold in back, from left needle, from cn.

LT (1K over 1P Left Cross): Sl 1 st to cn and hold in front, p1 from left needle, k1 tbl from cn.

RC dec (1 over 1 Right Cross decrease): Sl 1 st to cn and hold in back, k2tog from left needle, k1 tbl from cn.

Body

With circ needle, CO 190 sts using the Cable Cast-On method (see Techniques). Place marker (pm) and join for working in rnds.

Border

Rnds 1–9: Knit.

Rnd 10: P4, k2 tbl, *p8, k2 tbl; rep from * to last 4 sts, p4.

Rnd 11: K3, RC, LC, *k6, RC, LC; rep from * to last 3 sts, k3.

Rnd 12: K3, k1 tbl, k2, k1 tbl *k6, k1 tbl, k2, k1 tbl; rep from * to last 3 sts, k3.

Rnds 13–19: Knit.

Knit 2 rnds.

Next rnd: K95, pm, k95.

Next (dec) rnd: K1, ssk, knit to 3 sts before next m, k2tog, k1, sm, k1, ssk, knit to last 3 sts, k2tog, k1— 4 sts dec'd.

Knit 11 rnds even.

Rep dec rnd—4 sts dec'd.

Knit 2 rnds even.

Next rnd: K29, work Row 1 of Border Chart over next 33 sts, then knit to end of rnd.

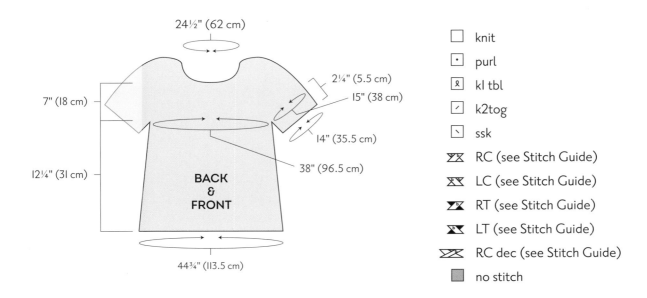

□	knit
·	purl
⅋	k1 tbl
⟋	k2tog
⟍	ssk
RC	RC (see Stitch Guide)
LC	LC (see Stitch Guide)
RT	RT (see Stitch Guide)
LT	LT (see Stitch Guide)
RC dec	RC dec (see Stitch Guide)
▨	no stitch

BORDER

33 sts

Cont as established through Rnd 14 of Chart 1 and *at the same time*, rep dec rnd every 12 rnds 3 times more—161 sts (76 sts for front, and 85 sts for back).

When Chart 1 is complete, cont in St st over all sts until piece measures 13¾" (35 cm) from beg. Set aside.

Sleeves (make 2 the same)

With dpn, CO 60 sts. Pm and join for working in rnds.

RNDS 1–9: Knit.

RND 10: P4, k2 tbl, *p8, k2 tbl; rep from * to last 4 sts, p4.

RND 11: K3, RC, LC, *k6, RC, LC; rep from * to last 3 sts, k3.

RND 12: K3, k1 tbl, k2, k1 tbl *k6, k1 tbl, k2, k1 tbl; rep from * to last 3 sts, k3.

RNDS 13–21: Knit.

NEXT (INC) RND: K1, M1, knit to last st, M1, k1— 2 sts inc'd.

Knit 2 rnds even.

Rep last 3 rnds once more—64 sts. Piece should measure about 4" (10 cm) from beg. Place first 2 sts and last 2 sts on holder—60 sts rem on dpn.

Yoke

With RS facing, place first 2 sts and last 2 sts on holder, knit held 60 sts for one sleeve, knit 72 front sts, place next 4 sts on holder and remove m, knit 60 held sts of rem sleeve, pm, knit rem 81 back sts—273 sts. Pm and join for working in rnds.

Knit 4 rnds even.

Next rnd: Knit to m at beg of back, k24, work Row 1 of Yoke Chart over next 33 sts, knit to end of rnd.

Cont as established through Rnd 5 of Yoke Chart—264 sts rem.

Cont even in St st over all sts until piece measures 19" (48.5 cm) from beg.

Next (dec) rnd: *Ssk, k6; rep from * to end of rnd—231 sts rem.

Next rnd: *K1 tbl, p2; rep from * to end of rnd.

Work 3 rnds as established.

Next (dec) rnd: (K1 tbl, p2tog) 18 times, k1 tbl, p2, k1 tbl, p2tog, (k1 tbl, p2) 15 times, k1 tbl, p2tog, k1 tbl, p2, (k1 tbl, p2tog) 40 times—171 sts.

Next 2 rnds: (K1 tbl, p1) 18 times, k1 tbl, p2, k1 tbl, p1, (k1 tbl, p2) 15 times, k1 tbl, p1, k1 tbl, p2, (k1 tbl, p1) to end of rnd.

Next (dec) rnd: (Ssk) 18 times, k1 tbl, p2, ssk, (k1 tbl, p2) 15 times, ssk, k1 tbl, p2, (ssk) 40 times—111 sts.

BO kwise, working into back of each st.

Finishing

Weave in ends.

Sew underarm seams. Fold bottom edge and sleeves to inside and sew to WS.

Handwash in warm soapy water, very carefully roll up in a towel, and gently squeeze out excess water. Reshape and leave to dry flat away from direct sun or heat source. On WS, press very lightly with a warm iron over a damp cloth.

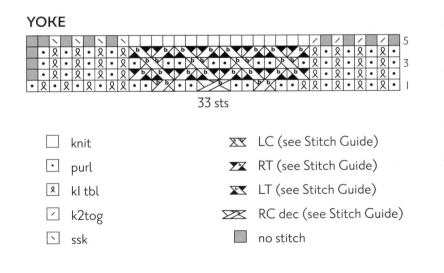

YOKE

33 sts

	knit
·	purl
ℓ	k1 tbl
∕	k2tog
＼	ssk

	LC (see Stitch Guide)
	RT (see Stitch Guide)
	LT (see Stitch Guide)
	RC dec (see Stitch Guide)
	no stitch

annikki slouchy hat

THIS HAT is an easy project for getting acquainted with the textural twisted- or traveling-stitch technique. These stitches have traditionally been used to give pattern and texture to folk knitting and can be found on many examples of long stockings, sock tops, mittens, and gloves. In this project, traditional twisted stitches are combined with rib stitches to give the Annikki Slouchy Hat a distinctively crunchy, nubby texture with enough stretch and positive ease to accommodate most women's heads. The Annikki Slouchy Hat is knitted in the round from the bottom up and is shaped subtly by gradually reducing the size of the double-pointed needles until the final stitches are decreased and finished with a "rosebud" gather.

FINISHED MEASUREMENTS
18" (45.5 cm) circumference and 11¾" (30 cm) tall.

YARN
Chunky weight (#5 Bulky).

Shown here: Hillesvåg Ullvarefabrikk AS Hifa Trollgarn (100% wool; 124 yd [114 m]/100 g): #7048 Marled Light Blue, 2 skeins.

GAUGE
18 sts and 22 rnds=4" (10 cm) in Twisted St Rib on largest needles, after washing.

NEEDLES
Size U.S. 9 (5.5 mm) 16" (40 cm) circular (cir).

Size U.S. 8 (5 mm) 16" (40 cm) circular (cir).

Size U.S. 7 (4.5 mm) 16" (40 cm) circular (cir).

Size U.S. 6 (4 mm) 16" (40 cm) circular (cir).

Set of 5 size U.S. 4 (3.5 mm) double-pointed (dpn).

Adjust needle size if necessary to obtain the correct gauge.

NOTIONS
Marker (m); cable needle (cn); tapestry needle.

LT (left twist): Slip 1 st to cn and hold in front, p1, k1 tbl from cn.

RT (right twist): Slip 1 st to cn and hold in back, k1 tbl, p1 from cn.

TWISTED STITCH RIB
(multiple of 6 sts)

Rnd 1: *K2 tbl, p1, k2, p1; rep from * around.

Rnd 2: *LT, p1, k2, p1; rep from * around.

Rnd 3: *K2 tbl, p1, k2, p1; rep from * around.

Rnd 4: *RT, p1, k2, p1; rep from * around.

Rep Rnds 1–4 for patt.

Hat

With cir needle, CO 79 sts using One-Color Fishtail Cast-On (see Techniques); do not include slipknot in stitch total. Join using Crossover Join (see Techniques). Place marker (pm) for beg of rnd.

Rnd 1: K2tog tbl, knit tbl to last 2 sts, k2tog tbl—78 sts.

Rnds 2–7: *K2, p1; rep from * around.

Work in Twisted St Rib until piece measures about 9¾" (25 cm) from beg, ending with Rnd 4 of patt.

Shape Top

Change to size U.S. 8 (5 mm) cir needle.

Work Rnds 1 and 2 of Twisted St Rib.

Change to size U.S. 7 (4.6 mm) cir needle.

Work Rnds 3 and 4 of Twisted St Rib.

Change to size U.S. 6 (4 mm) cir needle.

Work Rnds 1 and 2 of Twisted St Rib.

Change to size U.S. 4 (3.5 mm) dpn.

Next rnd: Work Rnd 3 of Twisted St Rib.

Next (dec) rnd: *RT, k2tog, p2tog; rep from * around—52 sts rem.

Next (dec) rnd: *K2tog, k1, p1; rep from * around—39 sts rem.

Next (dec) rnd: *K2tog tbl, p1; rep from * around—26 sts.

Next (dec) rnd: *K2tog tbl; rep from * around—13 sts rem.

Cut yarn, leaving an 8" (20.5 cm) tail, thread tail through rem sts, pull tight to close hole, and fasten off on WS.

Finishing

Weave in ends.

Handwash in warm soapy water, very carefully roll up in a towel, and gently squeeze out excess water. Reshape and leave to dry flat away from direct sun or heat source.

riita scarf

RIITA IS an ideal project with which you can explore the distinctively beautiful and textural Estonian nupp. In Estonian museum collections, there are many stunning and superb examples of large, finely knitted Estonian lace shawls that show off the use of the Estonian nupp wonderfully. The majority of these shawls would have been knitted in the coastal town of Haapsalu, where there was a tradition to knit fine lace. Often liberally incorporated into elaborate openwork lace patterns, nupps are quintessentially Estonian knitted bobbles and are made by wrapping the yarn around the needle either five, seven, or nine times depending on the required size and type of yarn used.

The Riita Scarf is knitted backward and forward with two needles in a fine laceweight yarn, and the nupps are made with nine wraps of the yarn. On completion, the scarf is washed in warm soapy water and left to dry flat, but not pinned or stretched.

FINISHED MEASUREMENTS
4½" (11.5 cm) wide and 82½" (209.5 cm) long.

YARN
Laceweight (#1 Super Fine).

Shown here: Tosh Lace (100% superwash merino wool; 950 yd [868 m]/4 oz [113 g]): Well Water, 1 skein.

NEEDLES
Size 2.5 mm (no equivalent; between U.S. sizes 1 and 2).

Set of 4 or 5 size U.S. 1 (2.25 mm) double-pointed (dpn).

Adjust needle size if necessary to obtain the correct gauge.

NOTIONS
Tapestry needle.

GAUGE
46 sts and 48 rows = 4" (10 cm) in 12-row lace repeat on larger needles.

42 sts and 48 rows = 4" (10 cm) in St st on larger needles, after washing.

9-STITCH NUPP
Working very loosely, work ([k1, yo] 4 times, k1) all in the same stitch—9 nupp sts made from 1 st. On the foll row, purl the 9 nupp sts tog (as shown on charts)—9 nupp sts dec'd back to 1 st.

Scarf

Tassels

*With dpn, CO 2 sts.

Work I-cord until piece measures 2¼" (5.5 cm).

NEXT ROW: K2tog tbl—1 st rem. Cut yarn, leaving a long tail, and slip st to a spare dpn.

Make 2 more I-cords the same.

Place all sts onto same dpn.

NEXT ROW: K3tog tbl—1 st rem. Set aside.

Rep from * twice more—3 tassels.

Place all sts onto same dpn.

NEXT ROW: K3tog tbl—1 st rem.

Body

NEXT ROW: CO 2 sts using Knitted Cast-On (see Techniques)—3 sts.

Work Rows 1–100 of Lace and Nupp 1—51 sts.

Work Rows 101–192 of Lace and Nupp 2—52 sts. Rep Rows 181–192 until piece measures about 67" (170 cm) from body CO, ending with a full rep.

Work Rows 169–179 once more, then Rows 128–168 once more.

Work Rows 193–220 of Lace and Nupp 3, then Rows 221–318 of Lace and Nupp 4—3 sts rem.

NEXT (DEC) ROW: Sssk—1 st rem.

Cut yarn and set aside.

Tassels

Make 3 tassels.

NEXT ROW: Place sts for tassels and scarf onto same dpn, k4tog tbl, fasten off rem st.

Finishing

Weave in ends.

Handwash in warm soapy water, carefully roll up in a towel, and gently squeeze out excess water. Reshape and leave to dry flat away from direct sun or heat source; do not pin or stretch.

On WS, press very lightly with a warm iron over a damp cloth.

LACE AND NUPP 1

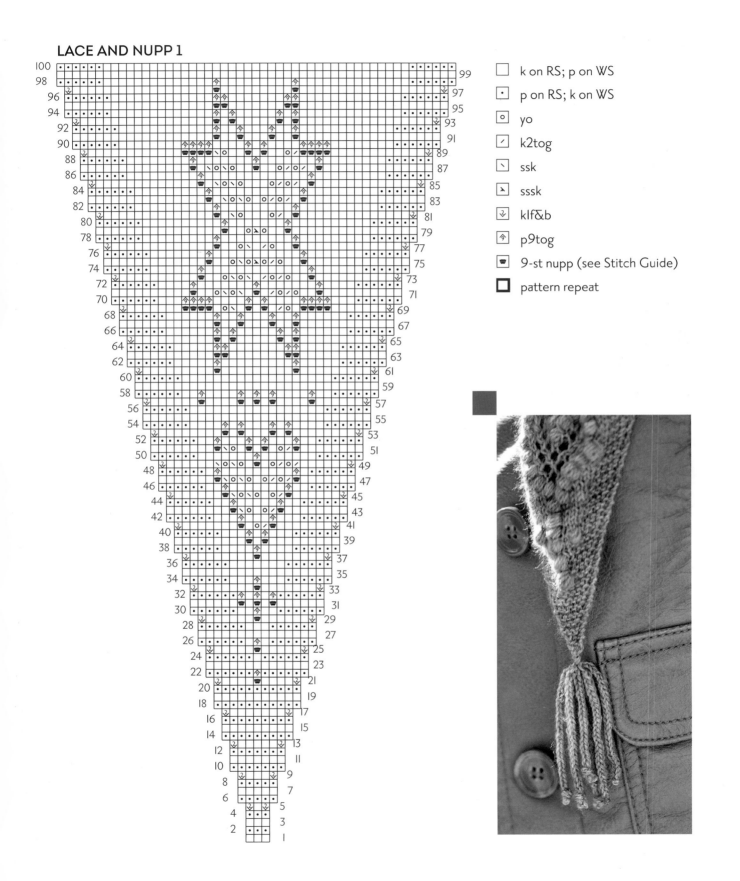

	k on RS; p on WS
·	p on RS; k on WS
o	yo
╱	k2tog
╲	ssk
⅄	sssk
↓	k1f&b
⇑	p9tog
⊍	9-st nupp (see Stitch Guide)
▢	pattern repeat

LACE AND NUPP 2

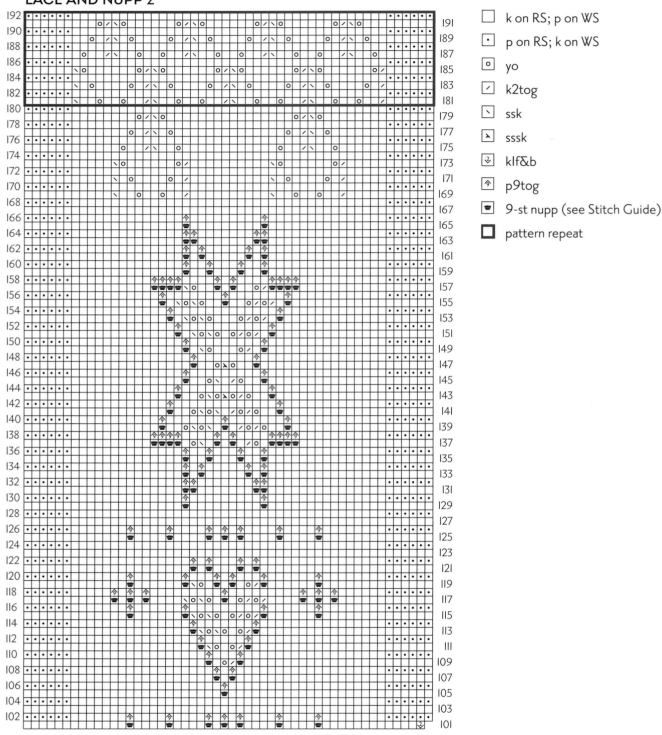

	k on RS; p on WS
·	p on RS; k on WS
o	yo
∕	k2tog
＼	ssk
↗	sssk
↓	k1f&b
↑	p9tog
♔	9-st nupp (see Stitch Guide)
☐	pattern repeat

LACE AND NUPP 3

LACE AND NUPP 4

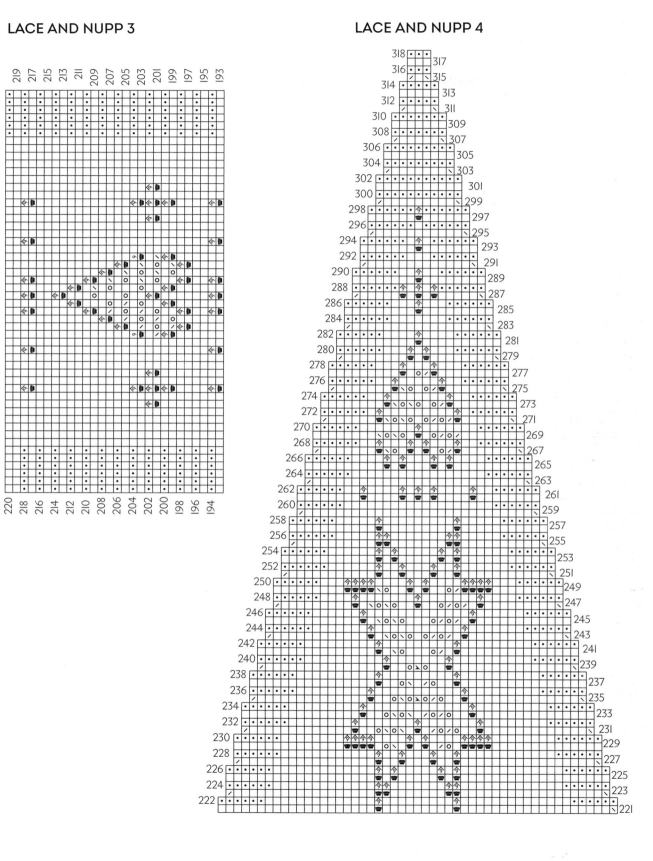

risto the squirrel

MANY TRADITIONAL mitten-making techniques have been used to give this toy squirrel plenty of character and charm. Risto is knitted in the round using five double-pointed needles, he has a decorative two-color braided cast-on, a twined purl-stitch band, stranded-colorwork patterning, peasant thumb openings for his arms, and decorative twisted-braid details. His fabulously bushy tail is also knitted in the round using five double-pointed needles and is decorated with traditional Estonian mitten fringes.

Risto the Squirrel is knitted in a chunky pure wool. Once he is completed, he should be washed in warm soapy water and left to dry flat. He is filled with a pure wool toy filler. Any weight of yarn can be used to knit Risto—you just need to follow the suggested gauge of whichever yarn you substitute with. If you were to use a finer yarn such as a Shetland four-ply, in a softer, sweeter color palette, a smaller Risto would make a very lovely toy for a baby.

FINISHED MEASUREMENTS
About 10" (25.5 cm) tall.

YARN
Chunky weight (#5 Bulky).

Shown here: Hillesvåg Ullvarefabrikk AS Hifa Trollgarn (100% wool; 124 yd [114 m]/100 g): #715 Brown (A), #717 Rust Red (B), #716 Soft Orange (C), #737 Natural (D), 1 skein each.

NEEDLES
Set of 5 size U.S. 9 (5.5 mm) each one 4" (10 cm) and two 8" (20 cm) double-pointed (dpn).

Adjust needle size if necessary to obtain correct gauge.

NOTIONS
Marker (m); holder; waste yarn; pure wool for filling; tapestry needle.

GAUGE
15 sts and 17 rnds = 4" (10 cm) in chart patt.

14 sts and 20 rnds = 4" (10 cm) in St st after washing.

Body

With longer dpn, and A and B, CO 45 sts using the Two-Color Fishtail Cast-On (see Techniques) with A on right needle and B on left needle; do not include slipknot in stitch total. Join using Crossover Join (see Techniques). Divide sts over 4 dpn. Place marker (pm) for beg of rnd.

Next rnd: K2tog A, (k1 tbl B, k1 tbl A) to end of rnd—45 sts.

Next rnd: Work in Estonian twisted braid (see page 75) p2tog A, (p1 B, p1 A) to end of rnd—44 sts. Distribute sts evenly over 4 dpn (11 sts on each needle).

Cut A.

Join C. Work Rnds 1–6 of chart 3 times. Piece measures about 4¾" (12 cm) from beg.

Arm Placement

Next rnd: Working Rnd 7 of chart, k8, knit next 6 sts with waste yarn, place these sts back on left needle, k6 with C, work 16 sts in established patt, knit next 6 sts with waste yarn, place these 6 sts back on left needle, k6 with C, then work to end of rnd in established patt.

Neck

Next rnd: Keeping unused yarns at back of work, *k1 D, k1 A, k1 B; rep from * to last 2 sts, k1 D, k1 A.

Next rnd: Keeping unused yarns at front of work and bringing new color up from under other colors, *p1 D, p1 A, p1 B; rep from * to last 2 sts, p1 D, p1 A.

Cut A and B.

Head

With D, knit 1 rnd even.

Shape Nose

Next (inc) rnd: Needle 1, knit; Needle 2, knit to last st, M1L, k1; Needle 3, k1, M1R, knit to end of rnd—2 sts inc'd.

Knit 1 rnd even.

Rep last 2 rnds 3 more times—6 sts inc'd.

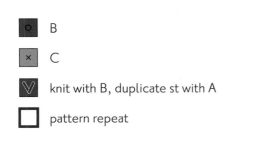

B

C

knit with B, duplicate st with A

pattern repeat

CHART

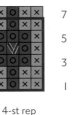

7

5

3

1

4-st rep
work II times

- -

NEXT (INC) RND: Needle I, knit; Needle 2, knit to last 2 sts, (MIL, kI) twice; Needle 3, (kI, MIR) twice, knit to end of rnd—56 sts (II sts each on Needles I and 4, and I7 sts each on Needles 2 and 3).

Knit I rnd even.

Turn work with WS facing. Working with a separate strand of D, join I3 sts each from Needles 2 and 3 using Three-Needle BO (see Techniques), sl next st from front needle and pass last BO st over slipped st, place slipped st back on front needle—30 sts rem (II sts each on Needles I and 4, and 4 sts each on Needles 2 and 3).

Turn work with RS facing. Cont in the rnd again.

NEXT (INC) RND: Needle I, knit; Needle 2, knit, then pick up and knit I st in gap above nose; Needle 3, pick up and knit I st in gap above nose, then knit to end of rnd—32 sts (II sts each on Needles I and 4, and 5 sts each on Needles 2 and 3).

Shape Face and Ears

Arrange sts evenly over 4 needles (8 on each needle).

Knit I rnd even.

Turn work with WS facing. Working with a separate strand of D, join 8 sts each from Needles 2 and 3 using Three-Needle BO, sl next st from Needle I and pass last BO st over slipped st, place slipped st back on Needle I—16 sts rem (8 sts each on Needles I and 4).

Turn work with RS facing. Arrange sts evenly over 4 short dpn (4 sts on each needle). Cont in the rnd again.

NEXT (INC) RND: Needle I, knit; Needle 2, knit, then pick up and knit I st in gap at forehead, Needle 3, pick up and knit I st in gap at forehead, then knit to end of rnd—18 sts (4 sts each on Needles I and 4, and 5 sts each on Needles 2 and 3).

Knit I rnd even.

Ear 1

Place 9 sts from Needles 3 and 4 on holder.

Next rnd: Needles 1 and 2, knit; Needles 3 and 4, using backward-loop method (see Techniques), CO 9 sts and arrange over the 2 needles—18 sts.

Knit 1 rnd even.

Next (dec) rnd: *K1, ssk, k3, k2tog, k1; rep from * once more—4 sts dec'd.

Knit 1 rnd even.

Next (dec) rnd: *K1, ssk, k1, k2tog, k1; rep from * once more—4 sts dec'd.

Knit 1 rnd even.

Next (dec) rnd: *K1, sssk, k1; rep from * once more—4 sts dec'd.

Next (dec) rnd: Sssk twice—2 sts rem.

Cut yarn, leaving a 6" (15 cm) tail, thread tail through rem sts, pull tight to close hole, and fasten off on WS.

Ear 2

Place held sts onto 2 dpn.

Next rnd: Join D at back of head, pick up and knit 9 sts along CO edge of Ear 1 and arrange over 2 more dpn, then knit to end of rnd—18 sts. Pm and join for working in rnds.

Make second ear same as first ear.

Left Arm

Remove waste yarn from first armhole and place the 12 sts onto dpn. Arrange sts evenly over 4 dpn (3 sts on each needle). Pm and join for working in rnds; beg rnds at back of opening.

Join B.

Knit 10 rnds.

Change to C.

Next rnd: *K1, p1; rep from * to end of rnd.

Rep last rnd 2 more times.

Paw

Change to D.

Knit 2 rnds.

Next (inc) rnd: K5, MIL, k2, MIR, k5—14 sts.

Next (dec) rnd: K1, ssk, k8, k2tog, k1—12 sts rem.

Next rnd: K1, ssk, k2, MIL, k2, MIR, k2, k2tog, k1—12 sts.

Next (dec) rnd: K1, ssk, k6, k2tog, k1—10 sts rem.

Next (dec) rnd: Ssk around—5 sts rem.

Cut yarn, leaving an 8" (20.5 cm) tail, thread tail through rem sts, pull tight to close hole, and fasten off on WS.

Right Arm

Work right arm same as left arm.

Tail

With longer dpn, and A and B, CO 25 sts using the Two-Color Fishtail Cast-On (see Techniques) with A on right needle and B on left needle; do not include slipknot in stitch total. Join using Crossover Join (see Techniques). Divide sts over 4 dpn. Place marker (pm) for beg of rnd.

Next (dec) rnd: K2tog A, (k1 tbl B, k1 tbl A) to end of rnd—25 sts.

Next (dec) rnd: Work in Estonian twisted braid (see Techniques), p2tog A, (p1 B, p1 A) to end of

After each fringe band has been knitted to the tail, turn work with WS facing and weave in ends. This will be much easier than trying to turn the tail inside out when completed.

Knit I rnd even.

NEXT (INC) RND: KII, MIL, k2, MIR, kII—26 sts.

Knit 2 rnds even.

NEXT (FRINGE) RND: Make a 26-st long fringe, and join to tail.

Knit I rnd even.

NEXT (INC) RND: KII, MIL, kI, MIL, k2, MIR, kI, MIR, kII—30 sts.

Knit 2 rnds even.

NEXT (FRINGE) RND: Make a 30-st long fringe, and join to tail.

Knit I rnd even.

NEXT (INC) RND: KI2, (MIL, kI) twice, MIL, k2, (MIR, kI) twice, MIR, kI2—36 sts.

Knit 2 rnds even.

NEXT (FRINGE) RND: Make a 36-st long fringe, and join to tail.

Knit 4 rnds even.

Rep last fringe rnd.

Knit I rnd even.

NEXT (DEC) RND: KI, ssk, knit to last 3 sts, k2tog, kI—34 sts rem.

rnd—24 sts. Distribute sts evenly over 4 dpn (6 sts on each needle).

Cut B.

With A, knit 4 rnds even.

NEXT (FRINGE) RND: With second set of longer dpn, B and C, cast on 24 sts using Fringe Cast-On (see Techniques) and alternating the yarns with each stitch. With RS of fringe facing (the braided/plait side), hold needle with fringe in front of tail, knit first st of both needles tog, (knit next st of both needles tog) to end of rnd—24 sts.

Knit 4 rnds even with A.

Rep last 5 rnds once, then rep fringe rnd once more.

Next (dec) rnd: K1, ssk, k11, k2tog, k2, ssk, k11, k2tog, k1—30 sts rem.

Next (dec) rnd: K1, ssk, k9, k2tog, k2, ssk, k9, k2tog, k1—26 sts rem.

Next (fringe) rnd: Make a 26-st long fringe, and join to tail.

Knit 1 rnd even.

Next (dec) rnd: K1, ssk, k4, k2tog, k1, k2tog, k2, ssk, k1, ssk, k4, k2tog, k1—20 sts rem.

Next (dec) rnd: K1, (ssk, k1) twice, k2tog, k2, (ssk, k1) twice, k2tog, k1—14 sts rem.

Next (dec) rnd: K1, ssk, k1, k2tog, k2, ssk, k1, k2tog, k1—10 sts rem.

Next (fringe) rnd: Make a 10-st long fringe, leaving 12" (30.5 cm) tails of B and C, and join to tail.

Cut A. Divide rem sts evenly onto 2 dpn. With 3rd dpn, join sts using Three-Needle BO (see Techniques). Weave in rem ends on tail.

Body Base

With longer dpn and B, CO 3 sts. Do not join.

Row 1 (RS): Knit.

Row 2 (inc): P1f&b, p1, p1f&b—2 sts inc'd.

Row 3 (inc): (K1, k1f&b) twice, k1—2 sts inc'd.

Row 4 (inc): P1, p1f&b, p3, p1f&b, p1—9 sts.

Row 5: Knit.

Row 6 (inc): P1, M1p, purl to last st, M1p, p1—2 sts inc'd.

Rows 7 and 8: Rep Rows 5 and 6 once—13 sts.

Rows 9–18: Work even in St st.

Row 19 (dec): K1, ssk, knit to last 3 sts, k2tog, k1—2 sts dec'd.

Row 20: Purl.

Rows 21 and 22: Rep Rows 19 and 20 once—2 sts dec'd.

Row 23 (dec): K1, ssk, k3, k2tog, k1—2 sts dec'd.

Row 24 (dec): (P1, p2tog) twice, p1—5 sts rem.

Row 25: BO and work (ssk) twice, k1.

Finishing

Weave in ends.

Embroider body foll chart. With A, work duplicate st for eyes, foll photo. With A, work a large bullion st at tip of nose.

EAR TUFTS: Cut 2 strands A, B, and C, each 4¾" (12 cm) long. Thread length of D in tapestry needle. Bring needle up through tip of ear from inside, hold short strands of yarn over tip of ear and bring needle back to inside and catch all short strands. Bring needle back to outside and wrap around the base of the short strands several times to secure and ensure that they stand upright. Bring needle back to inside and fasten off yarn on WS.

Handwash in warm soapy water, very carefully roll up in a towel, and gently squeeze out excess water. Reshape and leave to dry flat away from direct sun or heat source. On WS press all pieces very lightly with a warm iron over a damp cloth.

Stuff arms with pure wool so they hang at sides of body and are not overfilled.

Stuff ears, rest of body, and tail.

Sew body base to bottom of body with narrow ends at front and back. Make sure to catch the back of the braided CO sts so the braided CO remains visible at edge. Rep for tail. To keep the tail upright secure it to the body with a few strategically placed stitches.

Tail Base

With shorter dpn and B, CO 3 sts. Do not join.

ROW 1 (RS): Knit.

ROW 2 (INC): P1f&b, p1, p1f&b—2 sts inc'd.

ROW 3 (INC): (K1, k1f&b) twice, k1—7 sts.

ROWS 4–10: Work even in St st.

ROW 11 (DEC): K1, ssk, k1, k2tog, k1—5 sts rem.

ROW 12: BO and work p1, p3tog, p1.

Bryn Hat

THE BRYN Hat is a perfect companion project for the Broc Sweater, having the same decorative relief pattern consisting of nuppiline bobble stitches lying between twisted braids. For those of you who are familiar with Swedish tvåänststickat or twined knitting, and the twined purl stitch in particular, you will recognize that the Estonian twisted braid and a twined purl stitch round are worked in exactly the same way. One explanation for this could be that Estonia, and especially the Estonian island of Muhu, attracted many Swedish immigrants, and naturally, Swedish knitting techniques must have become integrated with the traditional Estonian techniques.

Quick to knit, the Bryn Hat is an ideal project with which to practice the nuppiline stitch and braiding techniques before embarking on a larger project such as the Broc Sweater. This hat is also knitted in a pure Shetland wool yarn, in the round from the bottom up, and there should be enough stretch and positive ease to accommodate most men's heads.

FINISHED MEASUREMENTS
About 21" (53.5 cm) circumference and 7¾" (19.5 cm) tall.

YARN
Aran weight (#4 Medium).

Shown here: Jamieson's Shetland Heather (100% wool; 101 yd [92 m]/50 g): #1000 Duck Egg, 2 skeins.

NEEDLES
Set of 5 size U.S. 9 (5.5 mm) double-pointed (dpn).

Adjust needle size if necessary to obtain the correct gauge.

NOTIONS
Marker (m); tapestry needle.

GAUGE
15 sts and 20 rnds = 4" (10 cm) in St st after washing.

NOTE
When knitting an Estonian twisted braid (which is worked in the same way as twined purl [see page 121]), both ends of the same ball of yarn are used, and I would recommend that you dedicate one ball of yarn specifically for the Estonian twisted braid.

Hat

With dpn, CO 80 sts using Cable CO (see Techniques). Place marker (pm) and join for working in rnds.

RNDS 1–7: *K1, p1; rep from * around.

RNDS 8 AND 9: Knit.

RND 10: Work in Estonian twisted braid (see page 75).

RND 11: Knit.

RNDS 12 AND 13: Rep Rnds 10 and 11.

RND 14: K2, p3, *k3, p3; rep from * to last 3 sts, k3.

RND 15: *K1, p2; rep from * to last 2 sts, k1, p1.

RND 16: P2, *k3, p3; rep from * around.

RND 17: Knit.

RND 18: Work in Estonian twisted braid.

RNDS 19 AND 20: Rep Rnds 17 and 18.

RNDS 21–23: Knit.

Shape Crown

RND 24 (DEC): *K8, ssk; rep from * around—72 sts rem.

RND 25: Knit.

RND 26 (DEC): *K7, ssk; rep from * around—64 sts rem.

Rnd 27: Knit.

Rnd 28 (DEC): *K6, ssk; rep from * around—56 sts rem.

Rnd 29: Knit.

Rnd 30 (DEC): *K5, ssk; rep from * around—48 sts rem.

Rnd 31: Knit.

Rnd 32 (DEC): *K4, ssk; rep from * around—40 sts rem.

Rnd 33: Knit.

Rnd 34 (DEC): *K3, ssk; rep from * around—32 sts rem.

Rnd 35: Knit.

Rnd 36 (DEC): *K2, ssk; rep from * around—24 sts rem.

Rnd 37: Knit.

Rnd 38 (DEC): *K1, ssk; rep from * around—16 sts rem.

Rnd 39: Knit.

Rnd 40 (DEC): *Ssk; rep from * around—8 sts rem.

Cut yarn, leaving an 8" (20.5 cm) tail, thread tail through rem sts, pull tight to close hole, and fasten off on WS.

Finishing

Weave in ends.

Handwash in warm soapy water, very carefully roll up in a towel, and gently squeeze out excess water. Reshape and leave to dry flat away from direct sun or heat source. On WS, press very lightly with a warm iron over a damp cloth.

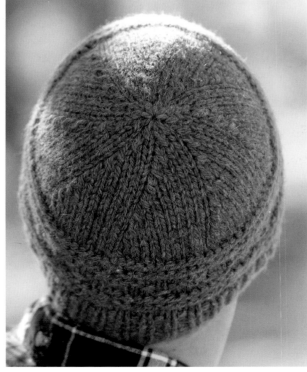

folk traditions

Knitting has always played an important part in the traditional folk costumes and customs of Scandinavia and the North, and it was the smaller items such as mittens, gloves, and socks that were in many ways considered the most important.

Often elaborately decorated and colored, these garments were integral to everyday existence, and were used not just as clothing but also as talismans—protecting the wearer from harm and bringing good fortune. Quite simply, it was believed that mittens had the power to protect the wearer, and in countries such as Estonia and Finland, they were even considered to have magical properties.

Mittens played a deeply important role in folk life, and as such, they would be worn on the majority of special occasions, even when sowing the first seeds of the season. It was a custom that when tending to sick animals the herbal medicine would first be strained, symbolically, through a mitten before the animal could drink it.

Traditionally, mittens, gloves, and socks, and the majority of sweaters would always have been knitted using five double-pointed needles—four to carry the stitches and one to knit with. It was also essential for a pure, unprocessed wool yarn to be used for knitted sweaters, as armholes and neck openings were often cut directly into the fabric. On completion, the sweater was washed, helping it to felt or full slightly before wearing and ensuring the cut stitches were definitely secure.

Wool offerings would be placed in chapels, and shepherds were often buried with a hank of woolen yarn on their coffin as a mark of respect. It was even common in Finland for the sheep to be blessed and then fed special little baked cakes.

broc sweater

T HE DESIGN for the Broc Sweater was inspired by both the traditional, textural one-color fishermen's jerseys, or "ganseys," and the Estonian Vatt, or knitted jacket. Traditionally Vatts were knitted by brides and given as gifts to their bridegrooms. Vatts were usually black and knitted in a textured relief pattern, or nuppiline stitch.

Although Vatts were traditionally knitted on two needles, felted, and then sewn together, I thought that the simplicity of the Broc Sweater would make an interesting and easy project in which to introduce the use of steeks. The steeks are incorporated as you knit and are then reinforced and cut to make the armholes. The Broc Sweater is knitted in the round from the bottom and has decorative Estonian nuppiline relief-stitch patterns between twisted braids at the lower edge and across the shoulders. It is knitted in a chunky pure Shetland wool, and the steeks are reinforced using a four-ply pure Shetland wool yarn.

FINISHED MEASUREMENTS
61¾" (157 cm) chest circumference and 27¾" (70.5 cm) long.

YARN
Chunky weight (#5 Bulky).

Shown here: Jamieson's Shetland Marl (100% Shetland wool; 131 yd [120 m]/3½ oz [100 g]): #126 Charcoal, 13 skeins.

Fingering weight (#1 Super Fine).

Shown here: Jamieson's Spindrift (100% wool; 115 yd [105 m]/25 g): #122 Granite, 1 skein (for reinforcing steeks).

NEEDLES
Size U.S. 9 (5.5 mm) two 16" (40 cm) and one 40" (100 cm) circular (cir) and set of 5 double-pointed (dpn).

Adjust needle size if necessary to obtain the correct gauge.

NOTIONS
Marker (m); holders or waste yarn; size 2 mm (no equivalent; between U.S. 1 steel and B-1) crochet hook; tapestry needle.

GAUGE
15 sts and 21 rnds = 4" (10 cm) in St st using larger needles, after washing.

NOTE
When working the Estonian twisted braid (see page 75), use both ends of the same ball of yarn. I would recommend that you dedicate one ball of yarn specifically for the Estonian twisted braid.

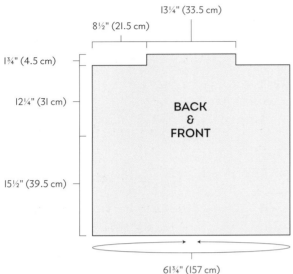

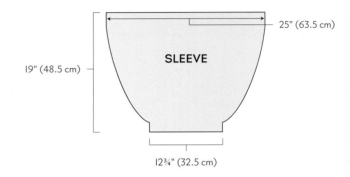

Body

With longer cir needle, CO 232 sts using Knitted Cast-On (see Techniques). Place marker (pm) and join for working in rnds.

Rnds 1–7: *K1, p1; rep from * to end of rnd.

Rnds 8 and 9: Knit.

Rnd 10: Work in Estonian twisted braid (see page 75).

Rnd 11: Knit.

Rnds 12 and 13: Rep Rnds 10 and 11.

Rnd 14: K2, p3, *k3, p3; rep from * to last 5 sts, k3, p2.

Rnd 15: *K1, p2; rep from * to last st, k1.

Rnd 16: P2, *k3, p3; rep from * to last 2 sts, k2.

Rnd 17: Knit.

Rnd 18: Work in Estonian twisted braid.

Rnds 19 and 20: Rep Rnds 17 and 18.

Cont in St st until piece measures 15½" (39.5 cm) from beg.

Armhole Steeks

Next rnd: K115, place next 2 sts on holder or waste yarn, pm, using backward-loop method (see Techniques) to CO 7 steek sts, pm, knit to last st, place last st and first st of rnd on holder or waste yarn and remove beg-of-rnd m, pm, CO 7 steek sts, place new beg-of-rnd m—242 sts (114 sts rem each for front and back, and 14 steek sts).

Cont in St st until piece measures 25" (63.5 cm) from beg.

Next rnd: Work in Estonian twisted braid over all sts.

Next rnd: Knit.

Rep last 2 rnds once more.

Next rnd: *K2, p3, (k3, p3) to 1 st before m, k1, k7 steek sts; rep from * once more.

Next rnd: *(K1, p2) to m, k7 steek sts; rep from * once more.

Next rnd: P2, (k3, p3) to 4 sts before m, k3, p1, k7 steek sts; rep from * once more.

Next rnd: Knit.

Next rnd: Work in Estonian twisted braid over all sts.

Rep last 2 rnds once more.

Neck

Next rnd: K32, pm, (k1, p1) 25 times, pm, k32, BO steek sts, k32, pm, (k1, p1) 25 times, pm, k32, BO steek sts—114 sts rem each for front and back. Set aside.

Sleeves (make 2)

With dpn, CO 48 sts using Knitted Cast-On. Pm and join for working in rnds.

Rnds 1–7: *K1, p1; rep from * to end of rnd.

Cont in St st. Change to shorter cir needle when there are too many sts to work comfortably on dpn.

Next (inc) rnd: K1, M1, knit to last st, M1, k1— 2 sts inc'd.

Rep inc rnd every other rnd 3 more times, every 3 rnds 6 times, then every 4 rnds 13 times—94 sts.

Knit 3 rnds even. Piece should measure 16¾" (42.5 cm) from beg.

Next rnd: Work in Estonian twisted braid.

Next rnd: Knit.

Rep last 2 rnds once more.

Next rnd: K2, p3, *k3, p3; rep from * to last 5 sts, k3, p2.

Next rnd: *K1, p2; rep from * to last st, k1.

Next rnd: P2, *k3, p3; rep from * to last 2 sts, k2.

Next rnd: Knit.

Next rnd: Work in Estonian twisted braid.

Rep last 2 rnds once more.

Next rnd: Knit. Place sts on holder or waste yarn.

Cut Armhole Steeks

Use the fingering-weight yarn and crochet method (see Techniques) to reinforce armhole steek sts.

Join Shoulders

Work a Three-Needle BO (see Techniques) on RS.

Join Sleeves

With shorter cir and RS facing, beg at bottom of armhole, pick up and knit 46 sts along side of armhole, then 46 sts down rem side of armhole, then knit 2 held sts—94 sts.

Return held sleeve sts to second short cir needle. Sl first st on left needle to right needle. Turn sleeve with WS facing and place sleeve inside body with WS held together and shaped edge of sleeve at bottom of armhole.

With RS facing, join sleeve to armhole using Three-Needle BO.

Neckband

With dpn or shorter circ needle, beg at left shoulder seam, pick up and knit 2 sts in left front neck edge, (k1, p1) across 25 held front neck sts, pick up and knit 4 sts in right neck edge, (k1, p1) across 25 held back neck sts, then pick up and knit 2 sts in left back neck edge—108 sts. Pm and join for working in rnds.

RNDS 1 AND 2: *K1, p1; rep from * to end of rnd.

RND 3 (DEC): *P2tog, work 50 sts in established rib, ssk; rep from * once more—4 sts dec'd.

RND 4 (DEC): Ssk, work 49 sts in established rib, sssk, work in rib to last 2 sts, p2tog—100 sts rem.

Work 13 rnds even in established rib.

BO loosely in rib.

Finishing

Weave in ends.

Fold neckband to inside and sew to WS.

Handwash in warm soapy water, very carefully roll up in a towel, and gently squeeze out excess water. Reshape and leave to dry flat away from direct sun or heat source. On the WS, press lightly with a warm iron over a damp cloth.

HÄRMÄ SOCKS

Härmä, **WHICH** means "frost" in Finnish, is a very fitting name for these lovely, thick and cozy socks as they are exactly what you want on your feet first thing on a chilly frosty morning. These socks are great for padding around the house and for wearing when warming your toes in front of an open fire.

Knitted from the top down using five double-pointed needles, the Härmä Socks have a traditional decorative cast-on, a deep rib, a typical half Nordic star pattern, a turned heel, shaped gusset, and classic toe shaping. Traditionally, the best mittens, gloves, and socks were adorned with a tassel. Sometimes the tassels would be made at the end of the fingers or the toe of a sock, which were of course slightly impractical but naturally symbolized that these were not for everyday wear but for special occasions and celebrations. The Härmä Socks are knitted in a chunky pure Shetland wool and once completed they are washed in warm soapy water and left to dry flat.

FINISHED MEASUREMENTS
10¾" (27.5 cm) foot circumference and about 10¾" (27.5 cm) long.

YARN
Aran weight (#4 Medium).

Shown here: Jamieson's Shetland Heather (100% wool; 101 yd [92 m]/50 g): #103 Sholmit (A),

2 skeins; #126 Charcoal (B), 1 skein; #1000 Duck Egg (C), tiny amount for embroidery.

NEEDLES
Set of 5 size U.S. 9 (5.5 mm) double-pointed (dpn).

Adjust needle size if necessary to obtain the correct gauge.

NOTIONS
Markers (m); waste yarn; tapestry needle.

GAUGE
15 sts and 22 rnds = 4" (10 cm) in St st worked in rounds after washing.

CHART

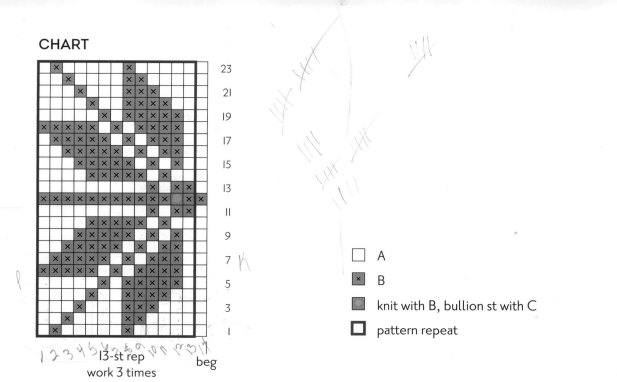

23
21
19
17
15
13
11
9
7
5
3
1

13-st rep
work 3 times

beg

☐ A

☒ B

▨ knit with B, bullion st with C

☐ pattern repeat

Socks

With 3 strands of B, use the Knotted Cast-On (see Techniques) to CO 40 sts—41 sts, including the slipknot. Cut yarns, leaving long tails to use for braided cord. Divide sts evenly over 4 dpn with 11 sts on Needle 1 and 10 sts each on Needles 2, 3, and 4. Sl last st on Needle 1 to Needle 4, pass last st CO over the slipped st and off needle—40 sts. Place marker (pm) and join for working in rnds.

Next rnd: With A, knit into the back of each st.

Next rnd: *K3, p1; rep from * around.

Rep last rnd 14 more times.

Knit 1 rnd.

Work Rnds 1–23 of chart. Cut B.

With A only, knit 1 rnd.

Heel

Next row (RS): K10, turn.

Next row: Sl 1, p19, turn. Place rem 20 sts onto one needle or waste yarn for instep.

Work back and forth on rem 20 sts for heel.

Next row (RS): *Sl 1, knit to end of row.

Next row (WS): Sl 1, purl to end of row.

Rep last 2 rows 3 more times.

Shape Heel

Row 1 (RS): K14, skp, k1, turn.

Row 2: Sl 1, p9, p2tog, p1, turn.

Row 3: Sl 1, k10, skp, k1, turn.

Row 4: Sl 1, p11, p2tog, p1, turn.

Row 5: Sl 1, k12, skp, turn.

Row 6: Sl 1, p12, p2tog, turn—14 sts rem.

Row 7: K7.

Gusset

With A and using dpn, Needle 1, knit rem 7 heel sts, pick up and knit 7 sts along edge of heel; Needles 2 and 3, knit across the held 20 instep sts; Needle 4, pick up and knit 7 sts along rem edge of heel, knit the rem 7 heel sts—48 sts.

Distribute sts if necessary with 14 sts (7 heel sts and 7 gusset sts) each on Needles 1 and 4, and 10 instep sts each on Needles 2 and 3. Pm for beg of rnd and join for working in rnds; rnds start at back of heel.

NEXT (DEC) RND: Needle 1, knit to the last 3 sts, k2tog, k1; Needles 2 and 3, knit; Needle 4, k1, ssk, knit to end of rnd—2 sts dec'd.

NEXT RND: Knit.

Rep last 2 rnds 3 more times—40 sts rem.

Arrange sts evenly over 4 dpn, with 10 sts on each needle.

Foot

Cont even in St st until foot measures 7¾" (19.5 cm), or about 2¾" (7 cm) short of desired length from heel.

NEXT RND: Join B, *k1 B, k1 A; rep from * around. Cut A.

Shape Toe

NEXT (DEC) RND: Needle 1, knit to last 3 sts, k2tog, k1; Needle 2, k1, ssk, knit to end; Needle 3, knit to last 3 sts, k2tog, k1; Needle 4, k1, ssk, knit to end—4 sts dec'd.

Knit 1 rnd even.

Rep last 2 rnds 6 more times, then rep dec rnd once more—8 sts rem.

Cut yarn, leaving an 8" (20.5 cm) tail, thread tail through rem sts, pull tight to close hole, and fasten off on WS.

Finishing

Weave in ends.

Embroider socks foll chart.

Braid long tails.

Handwash in warm soapy water, carefully roll up in a towel, and gently squeeze out excess water. Reshape and leave to dry flat away from direct sun or heat source.

Press very lightly with a warm iron over a damp cloth.

elsa sweater

T HE ELSA Sweater is knitted in the round from the bottom up, and all the decorative techniques used to construct the sweater have been inspired by traditional Nordic knitwear and in particular mittens and gloves. The sweater has a decorative two-color folk cast-on, a wavy scalloped border often found on mitten cuffs, classic Estonian nuppiline stitches, and a colorful vikkel band. All these techniques, combined with rows of classic lice stitch, give this sweater an unmistakable Nordic look. Traditional steeks are incorporated as you knit, which are then reinforced and cut to make the neckholes and armholes.

It is important that a pure wool yarn is used for this project as, once completed, steeked garments must be washed in warm soapy water to ensure the reinforced and cut stitches are secure. The generous, oversized proportions of the sweater, combined with a chunky pure wool yarn in a soft and subtle color palette, create a superbly cozy and cosseting sweater that is ideal for indoors or out.

FINISHED MEASUREMENTS
50¾" (129 cm) bust circumference and 25¼" (64 cm) long.

YARN
Chunky weight (#5 Bulky).

Shown here: Hillesvåg Ullvarefabrikk AS Hifa Trollgarn (100% wool; 124 yd [114 m]/100 g): #703 Light Grey (A), 10 skeins; #7048 Marled Light Blue (B), 2 skeins; #704 Mid Grey (C), 1 skein; #7040 Marled Green (D), 1 skein.

Jamieson & Smith 2Ply Lace Yarn (100% Shetland wool; 185 yd [169 m]/25 g): #L1A Natural White, 1 skein (for reinforcing the steeks).

NEEDLES
Size U.S. 9 (5.5 mm) two 16" (40 cm) and one 32" (80 cm) or longer circular (cir) and set of 5 double-pointed (dpn).

Adjust needle size if necessary to obtain the correct gauge.

NOTIONS
Markers (m); holders or waste yarn; size 2 mm (no equivalent; between U.S. 1 steel and B-1) crochet hook; tapestry needle.

GAUGE
14½ sts and 19 rnds = 4" (10 cm) in chart patt after washing.

14 sts and 21 rnds = 4" (10 cm) in St st after washing.

stitch guide

SCALLOP PATTERN
(multiple of 12 sts)

Rnd 1: *K1, yo, k3, k2tog, p1, ssk, k3, yo; rep from * around.

Rnd 2: *K6, p1, k5; rep from * around.

Rep Rnds 1 and 2 for patt.

Note: When working the scallop pattern at bottom of body, do not cut color A when changing colors. Leave A at the back of the work and pick it up again after working two rounds with the second color.

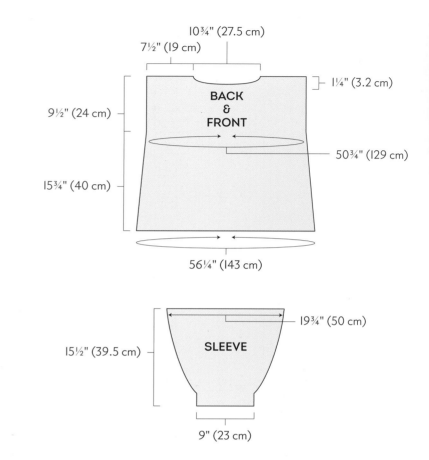

Body

With longer cir, and B and C, CO 205 sts using the Two-Color Fishtail Cast-On (see Techniques) with B on right needle and C on left needle; do not include slipknot in stitch total. Cut B and C.

Row 1: Join A, k2tog tbl, then knit tbl to end of row. Do not turn. Place marker (pm) and join for working in rnds.

Rnd 2 (dec): P2tog, then purl to end of rnd— 204 sts.

Rnd 3: Knit.

Rnds 4–9: Work Scallop patt Rnds 1 and 2 three times.

Rnds 10 and 11: Join C and work 2 rnds in patt. Cut C.

Rnd 12: With A, work 1 rnd in patt.

Rnds 13 and 14: Join D and work 2 rnds in patt. Cut D.

Rnd 15: With A, work 1 rnd in patt.

Rnds 16 and 17: Join B and work 2 rnds in patt.

Rnd 18: Join A and work 1 rnd in patt.

Rnd 19: Work in Estonian twisted braid (see Techniques).

Rnd 20: Join B and C. Keeping unused yarn at back of work, *k1 tbl A, k1 tbl C, k1 tbl B; rep from * to end of rnd.

BODY

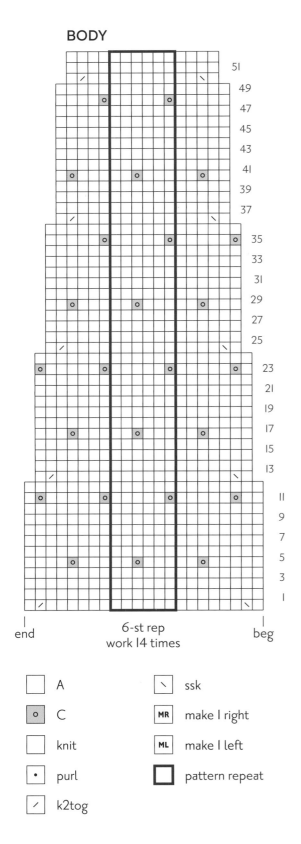

end · 6-st rep work 14 times · beg

	A			ssk
○	C		MR	make 1 right
	knit		ML	make 1 left
•	purl			pattern repeat
╱	k2tog			

RND 21: Keeping unused yarn at back of work, *pl tbl A, pl tbl C, pl tbl B; rep from * to end of rnd. Cut B and C.

RND 22: With A, k102 pm, knit to end of rnd.

Work Rnd 1 of Body chart as foll: *work 8 sts before rep, work 6-st rep 14 times, work 8 sts after rep; rep from * once more—4 sts dec'd.

Work Rnds 2–53 of chart as established—184 sts. Piece should measure 15¾" (40 cm) from beg.

Armhole Steeks

NEXT RND: K91, place next 2 sts on holder or waste yarn and remove side m, pm, use backward-loop method (see Techniques) to CO 7 steek sts, pm, knit to last st, pm, place last st and first st of rnd on holder or waste yarn and remove beg-of-rnd m, use backward-loop method to CO 7 steek sts, place new beg-of-rnd m—194 sts (90 sts rem each for front and back, and 14 steek sts).

Cont even until piece measures 24" (61 cm) from beg.

Shape Neck

NEXT RND: K30, place next 30 sts on holder, use backward loop method to CO 7 steek sts, k67 (next 30 sts, 7 steek sts, then next 30 sts), place next 30 sts on holder, CO 7 steek sts, knit to end of rnd—148 sts (60 sts rem each for front and back, and 28 steek sts).

NEXT (DEC) RND: *Knit to 5 sts before neck steek, (ssk) twice, k1, k7 steek sts, k1, (k2tog) twice; rep from * once more, then knit to end of rnd—8 sts dec'd.

Knit 1 rnd even.

Rep dec rnd—132 sts (52 sts rem each for front and back, and 28 steek sts).

Knit 1 rnd even.

SLEEVE

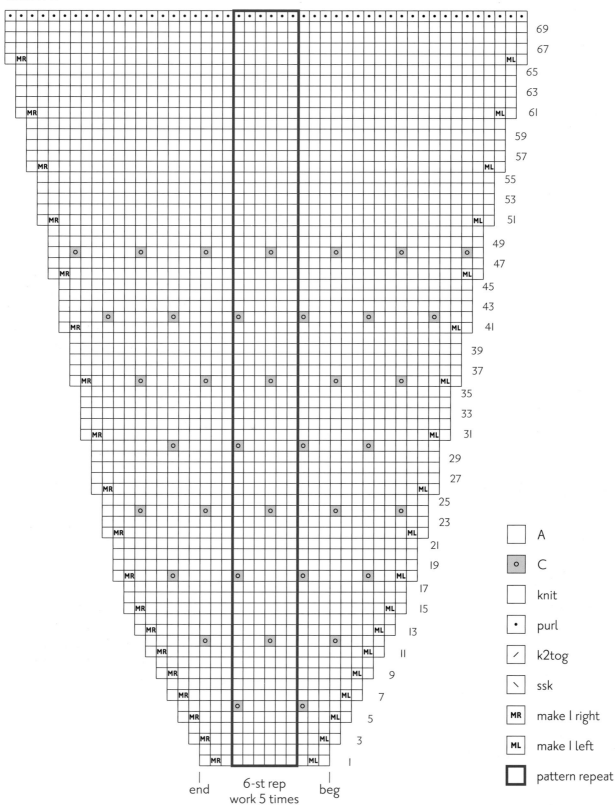

69
67
65
63
61
59
57
55
53
51
49
47
45
43
41
39
37
35
33
31
29
27
25
23
21
19
17
15
13
11
9
7
5
3
1

| end | 6-st rep work 5 times | beg |

	A
⊙	C
	knit
•	purl
╱	k2tog
╲	ssk
MR	make 1 right
ML	make 1 left
	pattern repeat

Next rnd: Knit and BO all steek sts—26 sts rem for each shoulder. Piece should measure 25¼" (64 cm) from beg. Set aside.

Sleeves (make 2 the same)

With dpn, and B and C, CO 34 sts using the Two-Color Cast-On (see Techniques) with B on right needle and C on left needle; do not include slipknot in stitch total. Cut B and C. Distribute sts over 4 dpn. Pm and join for working in rnds.

Rnd 1: Join A, knit tbl in each st to last 2 sts, k2tog tbl.

Rnd 2 (dec): P2tog, purl to end of rnd—33 sts.

Rnd 3: Knit.

Rnds 4–8: *K2, p1; rep from * around.

Rnd 9 (inc): *K2, p1; rep to last 3 sts, k2, M1, p1—34 sts.

Work Rnds 1–70 of Sleeve chart—72 sts. Change to shorter cir needle when there are too many sts to work comfortably on dpn. Place sts on holder or waste yarn.

Cut Armhole Steeks

Use the laceweight yarn and crochet method to reinforce steek sts around armholes (see Techniques).

Join Shoulders

Join shoulders using Three-Needle BO (see Techniques) on WS.

Join Sleeves

With shorter cir, A, and RS facing, beg at bottom of armhole, pick up and knit 35 sts along side of armhole to shoulder seam, 35 sts down rem side of armhole, then knit 2 held sts —72 sts.

Return held sleeve sts to second short cir needle. Turn sleeve with WS facing and place sleeve inside body with WS held together and shaped edge of sleeve at bottom of armhole.

With RS facing, join sleeve to armhole using Three-Needle BO.

Cut Neck Steeks

Use the laceweight yarn and crochet method to reinforce steek sts around neck.

Neckband

With shorter cir needle, A and with RS facing, beg at left shoulder seam, pick up and knit 6 sts along left front neck, knit held 30 front sts, pick up and knit 12 sts along right neck edge, knit held 30 back sts, then pick up and knit 6 sts along left back neck—84 sts. Pm and join for working in rnds.

Rnd 1: *K2, p1; rep from * around.

Rnds 2–28: Rep Rnd 1.

BO loosely in rib.

Finishing

Fold neckband to WS and sew to neck edge; make sure cut steeks are covered.

Weave in ends.

Handwash in warm soapy water, very carefully roll up in a towel, and gently squeeze out excess water. Reshape and leave to dry flat away from direct sun or heat source. On the WS, press very lightly with a warm iron over a damp cloth.

fia plötulopi cardigan

SATISFYINGLY SIMPLE and straightforward, this project is an ideal opportunity to experience knitting with the exceptional pure wool Plötulopi. This ethereal Icelandic yarn is both sumptuously warm and wonderfully fuzzy—think of arctic hares and foxes and you can begin to imagine what it is like to wear the Fia cardigan. The yoke is given a slight gathered effect reminiscent of traditional peasant blouses, and the simple lace stitch and garter-stitch border are both stitches commonly found in traditional Nordic and Icelandic knitwear, and mittens in particular.

Some care must be taken when working with this yarn (which is used double throughout), as it is surprisingly fragile. If you are using it for the first time, I would recommend that you knit a practice swatch before embarking on the whole cardigan. It is also essential that once the garment is completed it is carefully washed in warm soapy water and blocked. Then, and only then, will the full beauty of the Plötulopi yarn be revealed.

FINISHED MEASUREMENTS
47¾" (121.5 cm) bust circumference with fronts overlapping and 26¾" (68 cm) long at center back.

YARN
Chunky weight (#5 Bulky).

Shown here: Istex Plötulopi (100% new wool; 328 yd [300 m]/3½oz [100 g]): #1038 Ivory Beige, 7 skeins.

Note: This yarn is very delicate and must be handled with care when knitting; be careful not to pull the yarn too hard and break it.

NEEDLES
Size U.S. 10 (6 mm) 32" (80 cm) circular (cir) and set of 5 double-pointed (dpn).

Adjust needle size if necessary to obtain the correct gauge.

NOTIONS
Markers (m); holders; tapestry needle.

GAUGE
16½ sts and 19 rows/rnds = 4" (10 cm) in Lace patt after washing.

LACE PATTERN
(multiple of 11 sts)

Row 1 (RS): *K1, yo, k3, k3tog, k3, yo, k1; rep from *.

Row 2 and all other WS rows: Purl.

Row 3: *K2, yo, k2, k3tog, k2, yo, k2; rep from *.

Row 5: *K3, yo, k1, k3tog, k1, yo, k3; rep from *.

Row 7: *K4, yo, k3tog, yo, k4; rep from *.

Row 8: Purl.

Rep Rows 1–8 for patt.

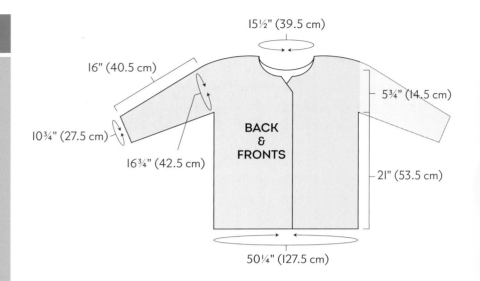

15½" (39.5 cm)

16" (40.5 cm)

5¾" (14.5 cm)

10¾" (27.5 cm)

BACK & FRONTS

16¾" (42.5 cm)

21" (53.5 cm)

50¼" (127.5 cm)

Body

With circ needle, CO 209 sts using Cable Cast-On (see Techniques). Do not join.

Knit 6 rows.

Next row (RS): K11 for garter border, place marker (pm), work Row 1 of Lace patt over next 44 sts for right front, pm, work Row 1 of Lace patt over next 99 sts for back, pm, work Row 1 of Lace patt over next 44 sts, pm, k11 for garter border for left front.

Cont as established until 8-row rep of Lace patt has been worked 12 times, ending with a complete rep. Piece should measure about 21" (53.5 cm) from beg.

Sleeves (make 2 the same)

With dpn, CO 44 sts using Cable Cast-On. Pm and join for working in rnds.

Knit 1 rnd. Purl 1 rnd. Rep last 2 rnds twice more.

Work Rnds 1–8 of Lace patt.

Next (inc) rnd: M1, work next rnd of Lace patt to end of rnd, M1—2 sts inc'd.

Working new sts in St st, work 3 rnds even.

Next (inc) rnd: K1, M1, work in established patt to last st, M1, k1—2 sts inc'd.

Work 3 rnds even.

Next (inc) rnd: K2, yo, pm, work in established patt to last 2 sts, pm, yo, k2—2 sts inc'd.

Work 3 rnds even.

Next (inc) rnd: Knit to m, yo, sm, work in established patt to m, sm, yo, knit to end of rnd—2 sts inc'd.

Rep inc rnd every 4 rnds 3 times, then every 8 rnds 4 more times—66 sts.

Cont even until 8-row rep of Lace patt has been worked 9 times. Piece should measure about 16¼" (40.5 cm) from beg.

Place first 3 and last 3 sts on holder for underarm—60 sts rem on needle.

Yoke

With cir needle and RS of body facing, remove markers as you work, k52 right front sts, place next 6 sts on holder, k60 sleeve sts, k93 back sts, place next 6 sts on holder, k60 sleeve sts, k52 left front sts—317 sts.

Cont in garter st, work 13 rows even.

Next (dec) row (RS): K11, k2tog tbl, (k3, k2tog tbl) 28 times, k3, k2tog tbl, k1, ssk, k3, (ssk, k3) 28 times, ssk, k11—257 sts rem.

Knit 5 rows even.

Next (dec) row: K3, k2tog tbl, k6, k2tog tbl, (k2, k2tog tbl) 29 times, k1, (k2, k2tog tbl) 29 times, k6, ssk, k3—196 sts rem.

Knit 3 rows even.

Next (dec) row: K3, k2tog tbl, k5, k2tog tbl, (k1, k2tog tbl) to last 10 sts, k5, k2tog tbl, k3—135 sts rem.

Knit 3 rows even.

Next (dec) row: K3, k2tog tbl, k4, k2tog tbl, (k1, k2tog tbl) 19 times, k1, (k1, k2tog tbl) 19 times, k4, k2tog tbl, k3—94 sts rem.

Knit 3 rows even.

Next (dec) row: (K3, k2tog tbl) twice, (k1, k2tog tbl) 13 times, k1, (k1, k2tog tbl) 12 times, k3, k2tog tbl, k3—66 sts rem.

Knit 1 row even.

Bind off kwise.

Finishing

Graft underarms using Kitchener st (see Techniques).

Weave in ends.

Handwash in warm soapy water, very carefully roll up in a towel, and gently squeeze out excess water. Reshape and leave to dry flat away from direct sun or heat source. On WS, press very lightly with a warm iron over a damp cloth.

snö mittens

THESE SNÖ Mittens were inspired by traditional Lovikka mittens and fittingly named after the Swedish word for snow. They are wonderfully cozy and insulating to wear; they are not only knitted in a pure wool, but have had pure wool thrums incorporated as they were made.

Famously, the first pair of Lovikka mittens were made "by mistake" in the small Swedish village of Lovikka, way up in the Arctic Circle. A young woman, Erika Aittamaa, spun some yarn and knitted a pair of simple mittens for a client, but the client was suitably unimpressed and rejected them. Luckily for us, Erika had a resourceful nature. Undeterred, she kept the mittens and rather than rework them, she washed, felted, and brushed them, and decorated the cuffs with bright embroidery. This new style caught on and the rest is history. These Snö Mittens have been designed to be roomy outer mittens, so you should be able to wear another pair of mittens or gloves underneath them.

FINISHED MEASUREMENTS
10" (25.5 cm) hand circumference and 9½" (24 cm) long.

YARN
Worsted weight (#4 Medium).

Shown here: LB Collection Pure Wool Yarn (100% wool; 180 yd [165 m]/3½ oz [100 g]): Natural (A), 2 skeins.

Fingering weight (#1 Super Fine).

Shown here: Jamieson's Spindrift Pure Wool (100% wool; 115 yd [105 m]/25 g): #425 Mustard (B), #1010 Seabright (C), #462 Ginger (D), #500 Scarlet (E), #525 Crimson (F), 1 skein each.

NEEDLES
Set of 5 size U.S. 6 (4 mm) double-pointed (dpn).

Adjust needle size if necessary to obtain the correct gauge.

NOTIONS
Marker (m); holder or waste yarn; tapestry needle.

GAUGE
21 sts and 26 rnds = 4" (10 cm) in thrummed St st in the rnd, unwashed.

THRUMS
Cut pieces of A, each 3" (7.5 cm) long.

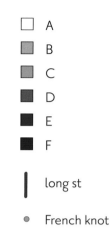

A
B
C
D
E
F

| long st

● French knot

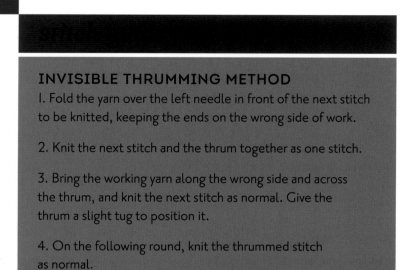

INVISIBLE THRUMMING METHOD

1. Fold the yarn over the left needle in front of the next stitch to be knitted, keeping the ends on the wrong side of work.

2. Knit the next stitch and the thrum together as one stitch.

3. Bring the working yarn along the wrong side and across the thrum, and knit the next stitch as normal. Give the thrum a slight tug to position it.

4. On the following round, knit the thrummed stitch as normal.

Right Mitten

Cuff

With A and dpn and using the Cable Cast-On method (see Techniques), CO 40 sts. Distribute sts evenly over 4 dpn. Place marker (pm) and join for working in rnds.

NEXT RND: Purl.

Knit 21 rnds.

NEXT RND: Purl.

Turn work so WS is facing.

NEXT RND: *K2, p2; rep from * around.

Rep last rnd 23 times.

Knit 3 rnds.

Hand

Next (inc) rnd: *M1, knit to end of needle; rep from * 3 more times—44 sts.

Rep last rnd 2 more times—52 sts. Adjust sts if necessary so there are 13 sts on each needle.

Knit 3 rnds even.

Next (thrum) rnd: K1, *k1 thrum, k3; rep from * to last 3 sts, k1 thrum, k2.

Rep last 4 rnds 2 more times.

Thumb Opening

NEXT RND: Needles 1 and 2, knit; Needle 3, k2, place next 8 sts on holder or waste yarn, using backward loop method, CO 8 sts over gap, knit to end of rnd.

Knit 2 rnds even.

NEXT (THRUM) RND: K1, *k1 thrum, k3; rep from * to last 3 sts, k1 thrum, k2.

NEXT (DEC) RND: Needles 1 and 2, knit; Needle 3, k4, k2tog tbl, k1, k2tog, k4, knit to end of rnd— 2 sts dec'd.

EMBROIDERY DIAGRAM

40 sts

21
19
17
15
13
11
9
7
5
3
1

■ ■

Next (dec) rnd: Needles 1 and 2, knit; Needle 3, K4, k2tog tbl, k2tog, knit to end of rnd—48 sts.

Knit 1 rnd even.

Next (thrum) rnd: K1, *k1 thrum, k3; rep from * to last 3 sts, k1 thrum, k2.

Knit 3 rnds.

Rep last 4 rnds 3 more times, or until hand measures about 4¾" (12 cm) above rib, or 1¾" (4.5 cm) short of desired length.

Work 3 more rnds in established patt.

Shape Top

Adjust sts if necessary so there are 12 sts on each needle.

Next (dec) rnd: Needle 1, k1, k2tog tbl, knit to end; Needle 2, knit to last 3 sts, k2tog, k1; Needle 3, k1, k2tog tbl, knit to end; Needle 4: knit to last 3 sts, k2tog, k1—4 sts dec'd.

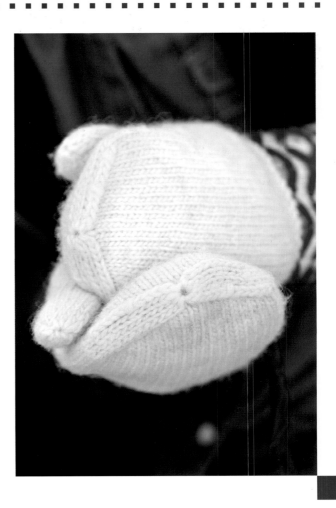

Rep dec rnd every rnd 9 more times, working a thrum rnd every 4th rnd as established—8 sts rem.

Cut yarn, leaving an 8" (20.5 cm) tail, thread tail through rem sts, pull tight to close hole, and fasten off on WS.

Thumb

Return 8 held sts to dpn, pick up and knit 8 sts along the CO sts above the opening—16 sts. Pm and join for working in rnds.

Knit 3 rnds even.

Next (thrum) rnd: *K3, k1 thrum; rep from * around.

Rep last 4 rnds 4 more times, or until thumb is ¼" (6 mm) short of desired length.

Shape Top

Adjust sts if necessary so there are 4 sts on each needle.

Next (dec) rnd: Needle 1, k1, k2tog tbl, k1; Needle 2, k1, k2tog, k1; Needle 3, k1, k2tog tbl, k1; Needle 4, k1, k2tog, k1—4 sts dec'd.

Next (dec) rnd: Needle 1, k1, k2tog tbl; Needle 2, k2tog, k1; Needle 3, k1, k2tog; Needle 4, k2tog, k1—8 sts rem.

Cut yarn, leaving an 8" (20.5 cm) tail, thread tail through rem sts, pull tight to close hole, and fasten off on WS.

Left Mitten

Work left mitten same as right mitten to thumb opening.

Thumb Opening

Next rnd: Needle 1, knit; Needle 2, k2, place next 8 sts on holder or waste yarn, using backward-loop method, CO 8 sts over gap, knit to end of rnd.

Knit 2 rnds even.

Next (thrum) rnd: K1, *k1 thrum, k3; rep from * to last 3 sts, k1 thrum, k2.

Next (dec) rnd: Needle 1, knit; Needle 2, k4, k2tog tbl, k1, k2tog, k4, knit to end of rnd—2 sts dec'd.

Next (dec) rnd: Needle 1, knit; Needle 2, k4, k2tog tbl, k2tog, knit to end of rnd—48 sts.

Cont same as right mitten.

Finishing

Weave in ends.

Turn mittens inside out so RS of cuff is facing.

Embroider cuff foll diagram, leaving 6 long tails (2 each of D, E, and F) at end opposite thumb for braiding a cord. *Note:* Long sts at each end of chart should be worked the full length of the other long sts.

Braid tails for cord.

Handwash in warm soapy water, carefully roll up in a towel, and gently squeeze out excess water. Reshape and leave to dry flat away from direct sunlight or heat source.

Press very lightly with a warm iron over a damp cloth.

Little tomte

THE SWEDISH and Norwegian Tomte (or Nisse as they are known in Denmark) live in forests, barns, or houses and are always easily recognizable by their distinctive red pointed hats. This particular little Tomte (he does not have a long white beard, so he can only be a young Tomte) is knitted in exactly the same way as a traditional Nordic mitten: in the round using five double-pointed needles, with a decorative braided cast-on, stranded-colorwork patterning, and traditional peasant thumb openings for his arms. His pointed hat has a twisted braid detail and is shaped in the same way as the top of a mitten.

Little Tomte is filled with pure wool, and his scarf is knitted separately, then tied and stitched in position. Any weight of yarn can be used to knit Little Tomte; you just need to follow the suggested tension of whichever yarn you use. A finer yarn will make a smaller Tomte, which would look lovely as a festive ornament.

FINISHED MEASUREMENTS
9" (23 cm) tall.

YARN
Sportweight (#2 Fine).

 Shown here: Dale Garn Heilo (100% Norwegian wool; 109 yd [100 m]/1¾ oz [50 g]): #5813 Mist Blue (A), #0020 Natural (B), #4018 Cherry Red (C), #9145

Asparagus (D), 1 ball each; #0083 Charcoal (E), #4203 Blossom (F), a small amount for embroidery.

NEEDLES
Set of 5 size 3 mm (no equivalent; between U.S. sizes 2 and 3) double-pointed (dpn).

Adjust needle size if necessary to obtain the correct gauge.

NOTIONS
Marker (m); waste yarn; pure wool for filling; tapestry needle.

GAUGE
24 sts and 26 rnds = 4" (10 cm) in chart patt after washing.

24 sts and 30 rnds = 4" (10 cm) in St st after washing.

Body

With A and B, CO 44 sts using 2 color Fish Tail Cast-On (see Techniques) with A on right needle and B on left needle); do not include slipknot in stitch total. Join using Crossover Join (see Techniques). Place marker (pm) for beg of rnd.

Next rnd: With A, k2tog tbl, knit into the back of each st around—44 sts. Arrange sts evenly over 4 dpn (11 sts on each needle).

Work Rnds 1–21 of chart. Piece should measure about 3¼" (8.5 cm) from beg.

Cut A.

Arm Placement

Cont with B only.

Next rnd: K8, knit next 6 sts with waste yarn, place these sts back on left needle, k6 with B, k16, knit next 6 sts with waste yarn, place these sts back on left needle, k6 with B, knit to end of rnd.

Face

Knit 17 rnds. Piece should measure about 5¾" (14.5 cm) from beg.

Cut B.

BODY CHART

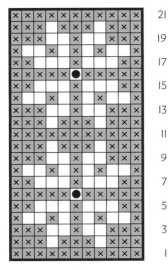

21
19
17
15
13
11
9
7
5
3
1

13-st rep
work 4 times

☒	A
☐	B
■	C
▨	F
⊙	knit with B, bullion st with C
☐	pattern repeat

- -

Hat

Join C.

Knit 1 rnd.

Work 1 rnd of Estonian twisted braid.

Knit 2 rnds.

Work 1 rnd of Estonian twisted braid.

Knit 1 rnd.

Shape Top of Hat

Adjust sts if necessary so there are 11 sts on each needle.

NEXT (DEC) RND: Needle 1, k1, k2tog tbl, knit to end; Needle 2, knit to last 3 sts, k2tog, k1; Needle 3, k1, k2tog tbl, knit to end; Needle 4, knit to last 3 sts, k2tog, k1—4 sts dec'd.

Knit 2 rnds even.

Rep last 3 rnds 8 more times—8 sts rem.

NEXT (DEC) RND: *K2tog; rep from * 3 more times—4 sts rem.

Cut yarn, leaving an 8" (20.5 cm) tail, thread tail through rem sts, pull tight to close hole, and fasten off on WS.

Left Arm

Remove waste yarn from first armhole and place 12 sts onto dpn. Arrange sts evenly over 4 dpn (3 sts on each needle). Pm and join for working in rnds; beg rnds at back of opening.

Join A and knit 1 rnd.

Shape Top of Arm

Short-row 1: Turn piece with WS facing, p6, w&t, k6.

Rejoin to work in the rnd again.

Next rnd: K6, lift wrap and place on left needle with next st, knit wrap and st tog, knit to end of rnd.

Knit 7 rnds even. Arm should measure about 1¼" (3.2 cm) along underarm.

Next rnd: Join B, (k1 A, k1 B) around.

Next rnd: With A, knit. Cut A.

Knit 4 rnds with B.

Shape Hand

Next (dec) rnd: (Ssk, k2, k2tog) twice—4 sts dec'd.

Next (dec) rnd: (Ssk, k2tog) twice—4 sts rem.

Cut yarn, leaving an 8" (20.5 cm) tail, thread tail through rem sts, pull tight to close hole, and fasten off on WS.

Right Arm

Remove waste yarn from rem armhole and place 12 sts onto dpn. Arrange sts evenly over 4 dpn (3 sts on each needle). Pm and join for working in rnds; beg rnds at back of opening.

Join A and knit 1 rnd.

Shape Top of Arm

Short-row 1: K6, w&t, p6.

Rejoin to work in the rnd again.

Next rnd: K6, lift wrap and place on left needle with next st, knit wrap and st tog, knit to end of rnd.

Work right arm same as left arm.

Base

With A, CO 3 sts. Do not join.

Row 1 (RS): Knit.

Row 2: Purl.

Row 3 (inc): (K1, M1) twice, k1—5 sts.

Rows 4–6: Work even in St st.

Row 7 (inc): K1, M1, knit to last st, M1, k1—2 sts inc'd.

Rows 8–11: Rep Rows 4–7—9 sts.

Rows 12–16: Work even in St st.

Row 17 (dec): K1, k2tog, knit to last 3 sts, k2tog, k1—2 sts dec'd.

Rows 18–20: Work even in St st.

Rows 21–24: Rep Rows 17–20—5 sts rem.

Row 25 (dec): K1, K3tog, k1—3 sts rem.

Row 26: Knit.

BO.

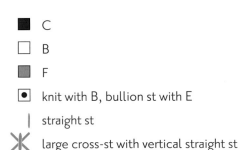

C

B

F

knit with B, bullion st with E

| straight st

large cross-st with vertical straight st

FACE EMBROIDERY DIAGRAM

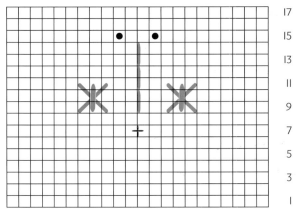

Scarf

With D, CO 10 sts. Divide sts over 3 dpn (3 sts each on Needles 1 and 3, and 4 sts on Needle 2). Pm and join for working in rnds.

Work in St st until scarf measures about 16" (40.5 cm), or desired length.

BO.

Cut 8 pieces of D, each about 3" (7.5 cm) long. Attach 4 pieces of yarn to each end of scarf for fringe. Trim to even length.

Finishing

Weave in ends.

Embroider body and face foll charts.

Cut 1 piece of A, B, and C, each 15" (38 cm) long. Thread one end of each piece in top of hat and secure on WS. With RS facing, braid a cord about 4" (10 cm) long. Knot end of cord.

Handwash in warm soapy water, very carefully roll up in a towel, and gently squeeze out excess water. Reshape and leave to dry flat away from direct sun or heat source. On WS press very lightly with a warm iron over a damp cloth.

Stuff arms with pure wool so they hang at sides of body and are not overfilled.

Stuff rest of body with pure wool.

Sew base to bottom of body with narrow ends at sides of body. Make sure to catch the back of the braided CO sts so the braided CO edge remains visible at edge.

Tie scarf around neck and take a stitch or two through ends below knot.

skogen twined scarf

THE SKOGEN Twined Scarf is a classic and stylish project that successfully combines the beautiful Swedish technique of tvåänststickat—"two-ended" or twined knitting—with two, tonal shades of yarn. As two ends of yarn are always used in combination for twined knitting—both the inner and outer ends of the same ball—this technique lends itself beautifully to blending colors. Madeline Tosh is renowned for her comprehensively sublime color palette, and I felt that the combined earthy, forest shades of Manor and Norway Spruce were evocative of the vast forests that cover great areas of many parts of the Nordic countries (Skogen is Swedish for "forest").

You can divide your ball of yarn into two separate colors, then as you start knitting, you will be using one end of each color. The Skogen Twined Scarf is a relatively easy project if you are new to the technique of tvåänststickat and a satisfyingly straightforward project if you are just wanting to indulge in all things twined.

FINISHED MEASUREMENTS
8" (20.5 cm) circumference and 72" (183 cm) long.

YARN
DK weight (#3 Light).

Shown here: Tosh Merino DK (100% superwash merino wool; 225 yd [206 m]/3½ oz [100 g]):

Manor (A), Norway Spruce (B), 2 skeins each.

NEEDLES
Set of 5 size U.S. 7 (4.5 mm) double-pointed (dpn).

Adjust needle size if necessary to obtain the correct gauge.

NOTIONS
Marker (m); tapestry needle.

GAUGE
26 sts and 22 rnds = 4" (10 cm) in twined knitting, after washing .

Scarf

With 2 strands of A and I strand of B, and dpn, use Twined Cast-On with Double Bead (see Techniques), CO 52 sts. Divide sts evenly over 4 dpn (13 sts on each needle). Place marker (pm) and join for working in rnds. Cut I strand of A; work with I strand each of A and B.

RNDS 1–3: *PI A; pl B; rep from * around.

RND 4: With A at back of work and B at front of work, work Crook St (see Stitch Guide) , but the round, as foll: *KI, PI; rep from * to end of rnd.

RNDS 5–7: (Using yarn A to knit Ist st, yarn B to knit 2nd st) knit

RND 8: as rnd 4.

RND 9-11: as rnds 1-3.

RND 12: as rnd 4.

RND 13: Knit.

Rep Rnd 13 until piece meas 70" (178 cm) from beg.

Rpt Rnd 4.

Rpt Rnds 1-3.

Rpt Rnd 4.

Rpt Rnds 5-7.

Rpt Rnd 4.

Rpt Rnds 1-3.

BO in twined knitting.

Finishing

Weave in ends.

Handwash in warm soapy water, carefully roll up in a towel, and gently squeeze out excess water. Reshape and leave to dry flat away from direct sun or heat source.

Press very lightly with a warm iron over a damp cloth.

abbreviations

beg(s)	begin(s); beginning		**pm**	place marker
BO	bind off		**psso**	pass slipped stitch over
cir	circular		**pwise**	purlwise; as if to purl
cm	centimeter(s)		**rem**	remain(s); remaining
cn	cable needle		**rep**	repeat(s); repeating
CO	cast on		**Rev St st**	reverse stockinette stitch
cont	continue(s); continuing		**rnd(s)**	round(s)
dec(s)('d)	decrease(s); decreasing; decreased		**RS**	right side
dpn	double-pointed needles		**sl**	slip
foll(s)	follow(s); following		**sl st**	slip st (slip stitch purlwise unless otherwise indicated)
g	gram(s)		**ssk**	slip, slip, knit (decrease)
inc(s)('d)	increase(s); increasing; increase(d)		**st(s)**	stitch(es)
k	knit		**St st**	stockinette stitch
k1f&b	knit into the front and back of same stitch		**tbl**	through back loop
k2tog	knit 2 stitches together		**tog**	together
k3tog	knit 3 stitches together		**WS**	wrong side
kwise	knitwise, as if to knit		**wyb**	with yarn in back
m	marker(s)		**wyf**	with yarn in front
mm	millimeter(s)		**yd**	yard(s)
M1	make one (increase)		**yo**	yarnover
oz	ounce		*****	repeat starting point
p	purl		******	repeat all instructions between asterisks
p1f&b	purl into front and back of same stitch		**()**	alternate measurements and/or instructions
p2tog	purl 2 stitches together		**[]**	work instructions as a group a specified number of times
patt(s)	pattern(s)			

techniques

Cast-Ons

Backward-Loop Cast-On

*Loop working yarn and place it on needle backward so that it doesn't unwind. Repeat from *.

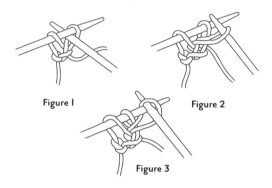

Cable Cast-On

If there are no stitches on the needle, make a slipknot of working yarn and place it on the needle, then use the knitted method to cast-on one more stitch—two stitches on needle. Hold needle with working yarn in your left hand with the wrong side of the work facing you. *Insert right needle *between* the first two stitches on left needle **(Figure I)**, wrap yarn around needle as if to knit, draw yarn through **(Figure 2)**, and place new loop on left needle **(Figure 3)** to form a new stitch. Repeat from * for the desired number of stitches, always working between the first two stitches on the left needle.

Figure I

Figure 2

Figure 3

Crochet Provisional Cast-On

With waste yarn and crochet hook, make a loose crochet chain about four stitches more than you need to cast on. With knitting needle, working yarn, and beginning two stitches from end of chain, pick up and knit one stitch through the back loop of each crochet chain **(Figure I)** for desired number of stitches. When you're ready to work in the opposite direction, pull out the crochet chain to expose live stitches **(Figure 2)**.

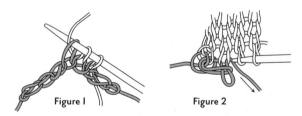

Figure I

Figure 2

Long-Tail Cast-On
(Continental Cast On)

Leaving a long tail (about ½" [1.3 cm] for each stitch to be cast on), make a slipknot and place on right needle. Place thumb and index finger of your left hand between the yarn ends so that working yarn is around your index finger and tail end is around your thumb and secure the yarn ends with your other fingers. Hold your palm upward, making a V of yarn **(Figure 1)**. *Bring needle up through loop on thumb **(Figure 2)**, catch first strand around index finger, and go back down through loop on thumb **(Figure 3)**. Drop loop off thumb and, placing thumb back in V configuration, tighten resulting stitch on needle **(Figure 4)**. Repeat from * for the desired number of stitches.

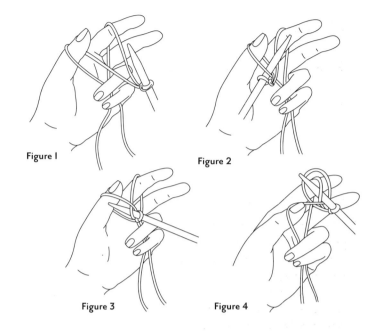

Figure 1

Figure 2

Figure 3

Figure 4

Twined Cast-On

Leaving long tails for braiding later, make a slipknot with two strands of A and one strand of B held together, and place the slipknot on the right needle; the slipknot does not count as a cast-on stitch. Hold B in your left hand and the two strands of A in your right hand **(Figure 1)**. Loop B around the left thumb and insert right needle tip into the loop as if to start a long-tail cast-on **(Figure 2)**, wrap one strand of A around the needle as if to knit, lift loop B over strand of A and off needle **(Figure 3)**, drop the B loop from the left thumb, and tighten the new stitch. *Loop B around left thumb again, insert needle tip into the loop, bring the strand of A farthest from the right needle tip over the previous strand of A used, wrap it around the right needle as if to knit, lift loop B over strand of A and off needle, drop the B loop from the left thumb and tighten; repeat from * until the required number of stitches are cast on, alternating strands of A and bringing each strand over the one used before. Break off B. Drop the slipknot from the needle before joining in the rnd, but do not untie it yet.

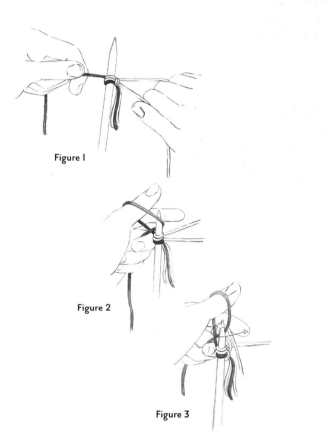

Figure 1

Figure 2

Figure 3

Twined Cast-On with Double Bead

Leaving long tails for braiding later, make a slipknot with two strands of A and one strand of B, and place the slipknot on the needle; the slipknot does not count as a cast-on stitch. Hold B in your left hand and the needle and two strands of A in your right hand **(Figure 1)**. Loop B around the left thumb. Slip the needle tip underneath both strands of the loop, between the loop and the web of your thumb (and not into the loop itself yet). Next, insert the needle tip down into the thumb loop from top to bottom **(Figure 2)** and rotate the needle so its tip is pointing upward again—the thumb loop now forms a figure eight, with the thumb and needle in separate compartments of the eight **(Figure 3)**. Wrap one strand of A around the needle as if to knit.

Insert the needle tip up into the thumb loop from bottom to top **(Figure 4**; this will undo the twist of the figure eight), drop the B loop from the left thumb, and tighten the new stitch.*Loop B around left thumb again, slip needle tip underneath both strands of the loop, then insert it down into the thumb loop from top to bottom. Rotate the needle so its tip is pointing upward again, bring the strand of A farthest from the needle tip over the previous strand of A used, and wrap it around the needle as if to knit. Insert the needle tip up into the thumb loop from bottom to top, drop the B loop from the left thumb, and tighten the new stitch; rep from * until the required number of stitches are cast on, alternating strands of A and bringing each strand over the one used before. Break off B. Drop the slipknot from the needle before joining in the round but do not untie it yet.

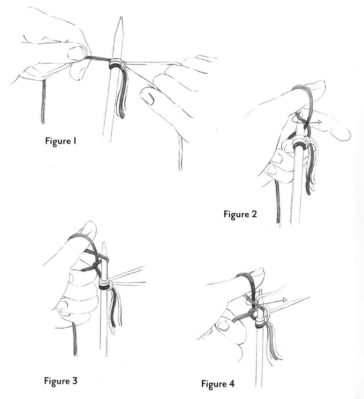

Figure 1

Figure 2

Figure 3

Figure 4

One-Color Fishtail Cast-On

This makes a braided edge with stitches pointing to the left. You will need two double-pointed needles.

1. Make a slip knot, leaving a long tail, and slip it onto the left needle.

2. With the right needle, knit one stitch into the slipknot, and keep it on the right needle. You have one stitch on each needle.

3. Bring the yarn from the back, between the two needles, and up in front, then over the top of the left needle, then, in a clockwise motion, take the yarn under the tip of the right needle to the back, then up over the top and around the right needle **(Figure 1)**.

4. Pull yarn through with the right needle to knit the stitch.

Repeat Steps 3–4.

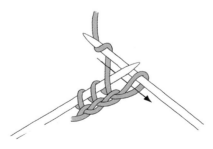

Figure 1

Two-Color Fishtail Cast-On

This makes a colorful braided edge with stitches pointing to the left.

This method is just the same as the one-color, only you make the slipknot using both colored yarns.

1. Make a slipknot, place the lighter-colored loop onto the left needle and the darker loop onto the right needle.

2. Bring the lighter yarn from the back between the two needles and make a stitch as before; the first two stitches are both light-colored.

3. Bring the darker yarn from the back between the two needles and make a stitch.

Repeat Steps 2–3 always alternating the yarns at the back of the work in an counterclockwise direction.

Fringe Cast-On

This starts just the same as the Long-Tail Cast-On but both sides of the loop around your index finger are picked up by the needle to make the fringe.

1. Make a slipknot leaving a long tail and slip it onto a needle. Hold the yarn from the ball around the index finger, and the long tail around the thumb — just the same as the Long-Tail Cast-On (see page 117).

2. Go to make your first stitch as you would for the Long-Tail Cast-On but take the needle behind both sides of the loop around your index finger.

3. Pull the needle through, use your index finger to maintain the fringe loop, and pull the long tail tight to secure the fringed loop.

4. Remove your index finger and set up again for the next fringe loop, keeping the long tail at the front of your work and the yarn from the ball at the back.

There will be two loops on the needle for each stitch cast on. Make sure to work both loops together for each stitch.

Knotted Cast-On

You will need two double-pointed needles.

This method is worked similar to the Continental or Long-Tail Cast-On but with a third length of yarn.

1. Holding both dpn parallel in your right hand make a slipknot and place it on both dpn.

2. Take another long length of yarn and hang it over the right needle next to the slipknot.

3. Pick up the yarns with your left hand taking one length of yarn around the index finger and three yarns around the thumb **(Figure 1)**.

4. Twist your wrist so that your palm is facing you and cast on the first stitch just as you would for the Long-Tail Cast-On **(Figure 2)**.

5. To cast on the second stitch, twist the front of your hand towards you and insert the tip of the needle under the yarn behind the thumb, bring the needle tip up to catch the yarn around the index finger, and pull the yarn through **(Figure 3)**.

Repeat Steps 4–5.

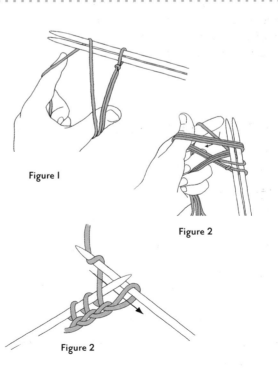

Figure 1

Figure 2

Figure 2

Bind-Offs

Three-Needle Bind-Off

Place the stitches to be joined onto two separate needles and hold the needles parallel so that the right sides of knitting face together. Insert a third needle into the first stitch on each of two needles **(Figure 1)** and knit them together as one stitch **(Figure 2)**, *knit the next stitch on each needle the same way, then use the left needle tip to lift the first stitch over the second and off the needle **(Figure 3)**. Repeat from * until no stitches remain on first two needles. Cut yarn and pull tail through last stitch to secure.

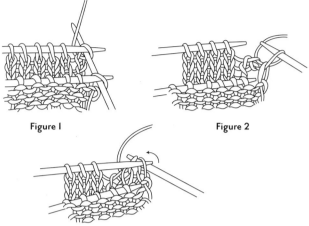

Figure 1

Figure 2

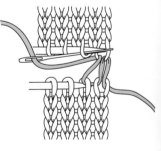

Figure 3

Grafting

Kitchener Stitch

Arrange stitches on two needles so that there is the same number of stitches on each needle. Hold the needles parallel to each other with right sides of the knitting facing up. Allowing about ½" (1.3 cm) per stitch to be grafted, thread matching yarn on a tapestry needle. Work from right to left as follows:

Step 1. Bring tapestry needle through the first stitch on the front needle as if to purl and leave the stitch on the needle **(Figure 1)**.

Step 2. Bring tapestry needle through the first stitch on the back needle as if to knit and leave that stitch on the needle **(Figure 2)**.

Step 3. Bring tapestry needle through the first front stitch as if to knit and slip this stitch off the needle, then bring tapestry needle through the next front stitch as if to purl and leave this stitch on the needle **(Figure 3)**.

Step 4. Bring tapestry needle through the first back stitch as if to purl and slip this stitch off the needle, then bring tapestry needle through the next back stitch as if to knit and leave this stitch on the needle **(Figure 4)**.

Repeat Steps 3 and 4 until one stitch remains on each needle, adjusting the tension to match the rest of the knitting as you go. To finish, bring tapestry needle through the front stitch as if to knit and slip this stitch off the needle, then bring tapestry needle through the back stitch as if to purl and slip this stitch off the needle.

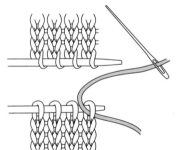

Figure 1

Figure 2

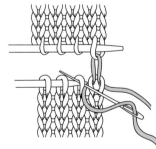

Figure 3

Figure 4

Special Stitches

One-Color Vikkel Braid

Vikkel is the Estonian word to describe patterns made with stitches that cross over each other, and this lateral braid is worked in a similar manner. The braids are not worked with an extra cable needle, but by manipulation.

One-color: Increase one stitch by picking up the bar between the last stitch worked and the next stitch, and knit into it through the back loop (this is the same as the MI increase). Place the stitch just made onto the left needle **(Figure I)**. *Bring the right needle behind this stitch, knit the next stitch through the back loop **(Figure 2)**, then knit the first stitch through the front as usual, and slip both stitches off **(Figure 3)**. Place the stitch just made back onto the left needle, and repeat from *. *Note:* Remember to always drop both stitches after they are worked. At the end of the round, pass the last stitch over the first stitch as to bind off to get back to required stitch count.

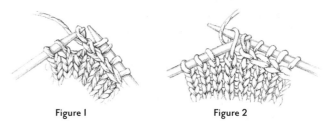

Figure I   Figure 2

Figure 3

Crossover Join

Join into a circle by moving the last stitch from the right needle onto the left needle and lifting the stitch to the left of the stitch just moved from the left needle, over the moved stitch and onto the right needle.

I-Cord (also called Knit-Cord)

Using two double-pointed needles, cast on the desired number of stitches (usually three to four). Knit these stitches, then *without turning the work, slide stitches to other end of needle, pull the yarn around the back, and knit the stitches as usual. Repeat from * for desired length.

Twined Stitches

Twined Knitting

*With both strands in back, insert right needle into next stitch on left needle as if to knit, bring the strand farthest from the tip of the right needle over the other strand, and use it to knit the stitch: repeat from * alternating the two strands and bringing each strand over the one used before.

Twined Purling

*With both strands in front, insert right needle into next stitch on left needle as if to purl, bring the strand farthest from the tip of the right needle under the other strand, and use it to purl the stitch: repeat from * alternating the two strands and bringing each strand under the one used before.

Intarsia in the Round

Round 1: Following the chart knit across the patterned area as normal, using both colored yarns.

Round 2: Work up to the patterned area as normal. Then, when knitting the motif, knit only the stitches of the main color and slip the pattern stitches (in the second color) purlwise onto the right-hand needle; these slipped stitches remain unknitted.

At the end of the patterned area, turn the work around so that you are now at the same place as you left the patterned yarn.

On the wrong side, purl, the stitches that were left unknitted from the previous round, with the pattern yarn only.

When the pattern is completed, turn the work again so that the right side is now facing you.

Now, slip the main color and patterns stitches across the motif and knit to the end of the round as normal.

Round 3: Work the motif as described in round 2 using both colors and then continue as normal with the main color until the end of the round.

- -

Increases

Raised Make-One

Note: Use the left slant if no direction of slant is specified.

LEFT SLANT (MIL)

With left needle tip, lift the strand between the last knitted stitch and the first stitch on the left needle from front to back **(Figure 1)**, then knit the lifted loop through the back **(Figure 2)**.

Figure 1

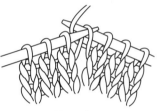

Figure 2

RIGHT SLANT (MIR)

With left needle tip, lift the strand between the needles from back to front **(Figure 1)**. Knit the lifted loop through the front **(Figure 2)**.

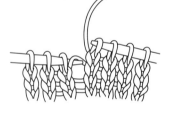

Figure 1

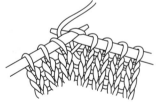

Figure 2

- -

Decrease

Muhu Decrease

Knit two stitches together wrapping the yarn onto the right-hand needle. Knit the next stitch wrapping the yarn around the needle in the normal way. Pass the twisted stitch over the knitted stitch. Two stitches are decreased.

Reinforcing Steeks Using the Crochet Method

Crochet steek reinforcements firmly bind together the sides of two adjacent stitch columns to hold the cut ends securely in place. The method is ideal for sticky or smooth animal fibers still at relatively dense gauges: the applied binding adds security even to yarns that don't felt readily, but it relies on a firm base fabric to stay in place. Crocheted steeks are not suitable for plant fibers or for superwash wools, since the base fabric must have some natural cling.

Regardless of how many stitches are used in the steek, a crocheted reinforcement is worked only on the three center stitches. Picture the two legs of the V formed by each knit stitch. For a crocheted steek, a line of single crochet binds together each half of the center stitch with the near half of the adjacent stitch. The left side of the steek (with the right side of the work facing) is worked first, from bottom to top. Then the right side is worked from top to bottom.

Figure 1

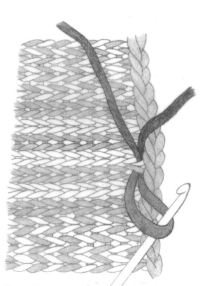

Figure 2

Begin by turning your garment sideways, so that you're looking at the steek with the cast-on edge on the right-hand side and the steek itself lying horizontally. Using a crochet hook of the same or slightly smaller diameter than the working knitting needles and a contrasting strand of the knitting wool, start at the cast-on edge and insert hook into the adjoining halves of the left-flanking and center stitches in the first row of the steek (**Figure 1**).

Yarnover and draw a strand of the reinforcing yarn through the two stitch halves (**Figure 2**). Yarnover again and draw the yarn through the loop, creating a single crochet stitch. Move on to the next pair of stitches above in the steek (or to the left as you look at the steek sideways).

*Insert your hook into the adjoining pair of "legs" in this pair, yarnover and draw up a loop (**Figure 3**). You'll now have two loops on your hook; yarnover and draw yarn through both loops, then move onto the next pair of stitches in the steek.

Repeat from * to the top edge of the steek; your steek should look like **Figure 4**. Cut the working yarn, and pull it through the last crochet stitch to fasten off. To work the right half of the steek, turn the work, start at the bind-off row, and work single crochet through the adjoining halves of the right-flanking and center stitches in the same manner, back down to the cast-on edge.

Figure 3

Figure 4

Embroidery Stitches

Bullion Stitch

Bring threaded needle out of knitted background from back to front. Insert needle a measure of distance away (the length of your bullion) and bring it back up at the starting point. Wrap thread around the needle a number of times as desired. Pull the needle through in an upward direction, adjusting the wraps as necessary. Reinsert the needle at the other entry point to tack down the bullion.

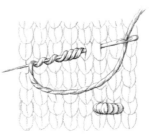

Cross-Stitch

Bring threaded needle out from back to front at lower left edge of the knitted stitch (or stitches) to be covered. Working from left to right, *insert needle at the upper right edges of the same stitch(es) and bring it back out at the lower left edge of the adjacent stitch, directly below and in line with the insertion point. Work from right to left to work the other half of the cross.

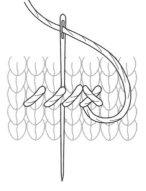

Duplicate Stitch

Bring threaded needle out from back to front at the base of the V of the knitted stitch you want to cover. *Working right to left, pass needle in and out under the stitch in the row above it and back into the base of the same stitch. Bring needle back out at the base of the V of the next stitch to the left. Repeat from * for desired number of stitches.

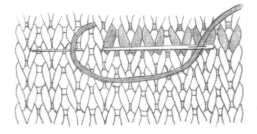

French Knot

Bring threaded needle out of knitted background from back to front, wrap yarn around needle three times, and use your thumb to hold the wraps in place while you insert the needle into the background a short distance from where it came out. Pull the needle through the wraps into the background.

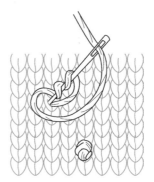

Straight Stitch

Bring threaded needle in and out of background to form a dashed line.

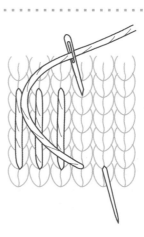

Sources for Yarns

Cascade
PO Box 58168
1224 Andover Park E.
Tukwila, WA 98188
cascadeyarns.com

Dale Garn
Distributed by Mango Moon Yarns
312 S. Elm St.
Owosso, MI 48867
mangomoonyarns.com

Hillesvåg Ullvarefabrikk AS
Leknesvegen 259
NO-5915 Hjelmås
Norway
ull.no

Ístex
PO Box 140
270 Mosfellsbær
Iceland
istex.is

Jamieson's of Shetland
Sandness Industrial Estate
Sandness
Shetland
ZE2 9PL
jamiesonsofshetland.co.uk

Lion Brand Yarn
135 Kero Rd.
Carlstadt, NJ 07072
(t800) 258- 9276
lionbrand.com

Madelinetosh
7515 Benbrook Pkwy.
Benbrook, TX 76126
madelinetosh.com

For my mother.

Once again I am deeply grateful to all at Interweave who have made this book possible.

I extend heartfelt thanks to everyone invoved, and especially to Francois, for all their expertise and support.

I have a considerable debt of gratitude to all the yarn companies who have so generously supplied me with wonderful woolen yarns. Many thanks indeed!

Index

take a scandinavian journey

THROUGH PATTERN AND COLOR WITH THESE INSPIRATIONAL RESOURCES FROM INTERWEAVE

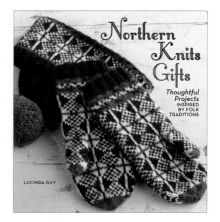

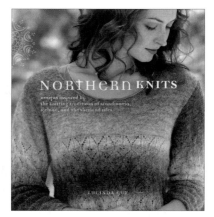

Northern Knits Gifts
*Thoughtful Projects Inspired
by Folk Traditions*
Lucinda Guy
ISBN 978-1-59668-562-8
$22.95

Northern Knits
*Designs Inspired by the Knitting
Traditions of Scandinavia, Iceland,
and the Shetland Isles*
Lucinda Guy
ISBN 978-1-59668-171-2
$24.95

150 Scandinavian Motifs
The Knitter's Directory
Mary Jane Mucklestone
ISBN 978-1-59668-855-1
$24.95

AVAILABLE AT YOUR FAVORITE RETAILER OR  SHOP.KNITTINGDAILY.COM

KNITS
INTERWEAVE

From cover to cover, *Interweave Knits* magazine
presents great projects for the beginner to the advanced
knitter. Every issue is packed full of smart, captivating
designs, step-by-step instructions, easy-to-understand
illustrations, plus well-written, lively articles sure to
inspire. Interweaveknits.com

knitting daily shop

Join Knittingdaily.com, an online community that
shares your passion for knitting. You'll get a free
e-newsletter, free patterns, a projects store, a daily
blog, event updates, galleries, knitting tips and
techniques, and more. Sign up at Knittingdaily.com.